Too Far Gone

An Addiction Memoir

A. T. MICALIZZI

FROG DUCK PRODUCTIONS
Philadelphia

Too Far Gone: An Addiction Memoir

By A. T. Micalizzi

Copyright © 2018 by A. T. Micalizzi, Frog Duck Productions

ISBN: 978-0-692-13822-9

For more about this author, please visit frog-duck.com or instagram.com/poemsbymic

1. Edited by: Dustin Schwindt
2. Cover by: Ronald Clarkson
3. Logo by: Andrew Arcangeli

First edition. March 20, 2018

To those that continue to fight a losing battle against their demons day in and day out: NEVER GIVE UP

CONTENTS

PROLOGUE

Addiction is a disease where a person compulsively abuses one or more substances until it negatively impacts their health and social lives. It disrupts lives, destroys families, and slowly kills its primary victim—the addict. In the U.S., addiction is an epidemic, and if we can all work towards understanding the nature of the addict, we can hopefully save their lives.

To the loved ones of addicts: First and foremost, they're worth fighting for. The toughest battle for a non-addict is the internal one. Almost every day, you have to remind yourself who they were and can be again, not who they've become. Remember that you are fighting for their lives. Insults will be thrown, tears will be shed, and you will be disappointed time and time again. But persevere because they are worth the fight.

It may seem nearly impossible, but voluntary commitment into a rehabilitation program on the part of the addict is the easiest method to ensure they receive the help they need. Contact the National Substance Abuse

Hotline at 1-800-662-HELP to seek out the best treatment. Check on your state's website for local help as well. With addiction being such a widespread problem, be mindful that openings can be tough to come by. Costs also can vary. Some health insurance policies cover addiction while others can cost tens of thousands of dollars. But don't lose heart. If you keep looking, you can and will be able to find treatment options that won't hurt your family financially. In most states, some level of involuntary commitment for addiction treatment is also allowed. With ample evidence to prove that the individual is an addict and a danger to themselves or others, he or she can be placed in a proper rehabilitation facility for a variable amount of time. Unfortunately, some states, including Pennsylvania, exclude addiction from their legal definition of mental illness causing involuntary commitment to be tough to achieve.

Currently, there are large gaps in the system when it comes to addiction, but the more we make our voices heard and help others to understand the devastation addiction causes, the better our options will become. Together, we can strengthen our current system so our loved ones have more and better options for treatment. In the meantime, we can utilize what help is available now. If he or she refuses to sign into a rehabilitation program and involuntary commitment is denied or doesn't work, there may be other legal options to force the addict's hand such as a restraining order. Call your local law enforcement to discuss immediate options in your area. If all else fails, plead with your loved one, convincing them of the beauty of life and love until you eventually break through. Never give up.

To addicts: You may have given up on your life, but you still love your family and friends. Find it in your heart and soul to listen to them. It may seem like an attack, but they have your best interests at heart. You can and will defeat this disease, but you can't do it alone. Use the resources available to you. Right now, you may be looking at your life and future through the hole of a straw. Sobriety will open your eyes and brighten your future once again.

Always remember, together we are strong, and we can defeat this.

Dear Mom:

You are my nurse when I am sick. You are my confidant when I need to talk. You are my cheerleader on the sidelines and my number-one fan. You are my teacher, my chef, my party planner. You are my motivational speaker. You are my mother and my best friend. You've always pushed me to be my best and supported me in trying to reach even my wildest dreams. You gave me strength when I was weakest, light in my darkest hours, and courage when I was most fearful. Now it is my turn to give that love back to you. I will be your confidant, your motivational speaker, your cheerleader, and your number one fan. You are fighting the toughest battle of all, but you will win. Just remember your own advice: "Mind over matter. You can do anything you set your mind to. 'Can't' is not in our vocabulary."

Love,
Anthony

To My Concerned Friends:

I felt it was finally appropriate to update everyone on the condition of my mom. I came home today for about one hour. Within that time, she screamed at and insulted me. She called my sisters and me "losers" and "mistakes." Her anger was unprovoked, yet familiar. None of this is surprising. After all, she is an alcoholic.

My sisters found out she has been texting close family and friends, letting out bits and pieces of our family's deepest secret, all while portraying herself as the victim. Frankly, that's unfair to my dad and to us.

My father is going through hell. For the past ten years, he has been involuntarily tasked with the nearly impossible job of keeping our family together while simultaneously keeping my mom out of trouble. During that time, she has been arrested twice, had three car accidents, and has been placed in the hands of the state twice. If not for my father, our family would be lost and broken.

The "abuse" my father apparently puts my mom through is a farce. Almost every night, my mother insults him relentlessly right in front of her children. She calls him fat and constantly brings up his ex-wife from over thirty years ago. Just today she told him, "I made the biggest mistake of my life marrying you." In addition to the verbal abuse, my mom threw away two wallets, broke two company phones, and took numerous trips to his work, attempting to get him fired (he brings in our family's only income). After all that, when she is sober, he still manages to tell her he loves her. His resilience is remarkable, but everyone reaches their limit, and we have reached ours.

In fear of my mental health, I have decided to move out on my own. If possible, my dad will take my sisters and I away for a short period of time. Aubrey is making plans to move "far away" once she graduates high school. Only fourteen, Angie has already started counting down the days until she can move away to college. The closest possible school is six hours away.

To an outsider, it may seem like we have given up on our mother. On the contrary, we have exhausted all options. Unfortunately, we cannot find a way to get her into a rehabilitation center, and she can't last much longer without it. To date, she has not attempted to commit suicide, but she has made threats. Without physical abuse or immediate fear of taking her own life, my mom has every right to stay home and continue to do what she does. Regardless of our planned interventions and video proof of the damage she has caused, she refuses help.

If we leave, my mom would not be able to take care of herself. She does not have her own income, and due to her constant drinking and lack of attention to her health, she would die on her own.

Addiction has gained full control of our mother and we are out of options. It is time for the truth to be told. Here is our story:

Part I

Dancing with the Devil

ONE

Family Business

"NO, please! Don't take her!" I scream, as my mom is slowly drug up the stairs. I chase after her, but I can't catch up.

My sister's scream, "Ant, please do something! Please save mom!"

I run up the stairs and find my mom crying as she is pulled her by her hair down the hallway and into her bedroom. I run with all my might to reach the door in time.

WHAM! The door slams in my face.

"Mom? Mom, are you okay?" I yell through the door. I try to open it, but it's locked.

"HA HA HA," a strange laugh bellows. "Your mom belongs to me! Nobody can save her!"

"Who are you? What do you want with my mom?" I yell as I look for a weak spot to break open the door.

"My name is no concern to you. Her time is up. I'm taking her with me," he announces.

I wind up to kick in the door—

BOOM! An explosion of light blinds me. I put my hands in front of my face and feel for my surroundings. A high-pitched ringing fills my ears as I attempt to call out for my mom.

When I regain my sight, the door is gone and I am standing just inside my parent's bedroom, staring at our family picture hanging on the far wall. In a trance, I walk towards it.

I scan all of the faces in the picture: mine, Aubrey's, Angie's, my dad's, and my mom's. Everything is the same. Then, my mom's face goes up in flames, and as quick as the fire starts, it is gone—her face now burned away. The ringing in my ears stops and that same deep voice whispers in my ear, "She is mine now."

I turn around, and my mom is gone.

I wake up in a cold sweat and anxiously look around the room, then sigh in relief. It was only a dream.

I check my phone and it reads ten o'clock Wednesday morning. With it being a day off work and summer break, sleeping so late usually means a fun night. Instead, I arrived home from college to our "normal" situation: my mom drunk again and belittling her family. My grandma, Palma (Dad's mom), had traveled an hour to visit us before we departed on our vacation to Disney World, so I traded in Zac Brown Band tickets for a night of "babysitting." When my grandma is around, we have to be extra careful my mom doesn't take her drunken anger out on her as she has done too many times in the past. Fortunately, on this night my sisters and I successfully kept our mom at bay. Nevertheless, I can't shake the dream I just had. I jump out of bed and walk straight towards my parents' bedroom.

"Mom? Are you in there? Mom?" I call out through the well-worn wooden door. Though she usually locks herself in her room, my mom always answers when I call for her. Not this time.

I put my ear to the door to see if I can hear anything as memories of the dream start rushing through my head. My palms sweat and my heart pounds in my chest. It's too quiet. I need to know she's okay.

I try calming myself with the thought of her in a heavy sleep. It doesn't help. I fear the worst.

"MOM! MOM! OPEN THE GODDAMN DOOR!" Again, no answer.

I contemplate breaking it down. I'm sure my dad will not be happy when he comes home to more splintered wood, but oh well. My mom's life is more important.

I take a deep breath, and just like the dream, I raise my leg to kick, but then I stop.

All around the door are reminders of our family secret: a patched-up hole on the right from one of my mental breakdowns (I try not to let my anger get the best of me, but it always turns ugly), another patched up hole in the middle of the door from when my father reached his breaking point (literally), and a chipped-out section of wood in the bottom corner from the first time my youngest sister experienced the unprovoked wrath of my mother. (Despite her small stature, her kick left permanent damage.)

But my mother has left the most damage. Her constant slamming of the door has left a broken frame and a crack down the middle. When drunk and angry (which is often lately), she lashes out at everybody: her friends, her sisters, her husband, and even her own children. Slamming the door gives her a sense of infantile empowerment.

The moment of reflection calms me down enough to remember my sister hid a key to my parent's room in her jewelry box.

I retrieve the key, head back to the door, and take another deep breath.

God, I hope she's just sleeping.

I turn the key and step inside.

I find my mom lying on the bed in the same baggy clothes she wore the day before, makeup all over her face, hair a mess. I check her breathing by watching for the rising and falling of the blanket. It moves. She's alive, but as usual, she is passed out drunk. My eyes go to the family picture hanging on the opposite wall. It is us on a "good day"—the day my sisters and I threw my parents a surprise party for their 25th anniversary.

My father, Elliot, stands in the back of the picture presiding over the family. At first glance, he resembles Tony Soprano—the typical brawny Italian-American with his slick, black hair and golf shirt tucked into dress pants. But the tattoos on his arms show where his heart lies. On his left arm, an Italian and an American flag represent our proud heritage. Above it, it reads "Aleutians" to commemorate my grandfather's service in World War II. On his right arm are his children's names in black ink. The tattoos reveal his big heart and his values: 'Love your family and never forget where you came from.'

Standing in the front of the picture are my sisters. Both of them inherited their looks from my mom: short and petite with long brown hair. Other than that, they are the complete opposite of one another. Aubrey is the consummate performer: acting, singing, and touring as a backup dancer for local musicians. When her high school guidance counselor asked her what she wanted to do after graduation, she responded, "Impressions." At seventeen, she developed my father's big heart and outgoing personality.

Angie is the quiet and reserved one, content to remain more invisible, but if she is comfortable around you, she is the exact opposite. She is by far the smartest in the family and has the strongest work ethic. Often found reading and studying, she aspires to graduate at the top of her high school class, attend a prestigious university, and become a neonatal nurse. At fourteen, she is becoming the spitting image of my mom, but unlike Aubrey, who wears her emotions on her sleeve, Ang holds hers in.

I stand behind my mother in the picture, the spitting image of my father. Like him, my family is everything to me, and I show it with my own tattoo on my back that reads, "La Famiglia Per Sempre" ("Family is forever"). As an aspiring teacher, I am outgoing and personable. When I am comfortable, I am loud and talkative, often dominating conversations. But more than any other trait, I am caring. I care for my sisters, my family, my friends, and the people around me. If I can help them in some way, I will every time. That characteristic I learned from my mom.

She stands in the middle of the picture with a big smile on her face—such pure happiness we don't often see from her. She's dressed in her nice designer clothes, wearing high heels and expensive makeup. Her long, brown hair is cut and combed, making her resemble the beautiful woman from my childhood.

I take one more look at the picture; it was the last time we were all happy.

I look down at the bed at Diane, a shell of my mother. I often try to disassociate the two, but lately, it has become harder. She is now ninety pounds, thirty pounds less than my mom's usual weight. Her hair more closely resembles a bird's nest, and she's missing a front tooth from when a drunken stupor caused her to lose her balance and her mouth met the side of a cement step. I try to remind myself of who my mother truly is. I need to remember who I'm fighting for.

In the past, my mom was strong-willed, intelligent, and the most selfless person I knew. She was once the manager of a multi-million-dollar company in the heart of Philadelphia. She always dressed in the nicest clothes, worked with business gurus, and held her own against anyone. She seemed invincible. More importantly, she was a loving mother who was heavily involved in her children's lives. She attended all school events, cared for us when we were sick, and dealt with our adolescent issues. I listen to all of her advice and ate up her encouragement.

Those who knew our family agreed that my mother was the nicest woman they'd ever known, and the hardest worker. My mom had a ton of friends and when they needed her, she was by their side without question. She did so much for others that she often forgot to spend time on herself.

Regardless of the occasional sisterly bickering, her sisters adored her, too. As the oldest sibling, she was the protector, and in some way, the matriarch. When her sisters needed anything, my mom was there for them. As young children, my sisters and I witnessed part of the special relationship she had with her family. We saw and felt how much everyone loved each other.

And my dad, he loved her so much. They had the kind of relationship many professional couples look for. During the week, they worked their asses off for their future, and on the weekends, they partied like the sun would never come up. Whether it was hanging out with friends or just the two of them, they had as much fun as possible. For the most part, they were inseparable.

After their weekly day of fun, they spent the remaining six days focused on their kids, and their love for us was unwavering. We did EVERYTHING together. Whether it was random trips to the zoo, a drive to the beach, a walk around Philadelphia, baseball games, softball games, cookouts, eating out at a restaurant, or just lazing on the couch watching movies, we did it all as a family.

But these little excursions were nothing compared to our family trips—the jam-packed fun-filled vacations we took each year. We planned them out for months and looked forward to them all year-long. We went to the Jersey Shore, Florida, Virginia, Delaware, and most often: Ocean City, Maryland. No matter where the next trip was, we looked forward to going there as a family. On vacation, we were the invincible "Fantastic Five." Nothing could touch us or bring us down...most of the time.

Now, the five of us spend the bulk of our time running away from "the monster," the code name we gave our mom for when she drinks. In her presence, family gatherings and dream vacations are nothing but a distant memory. Our reality lies before me in my mother's bed.

I sit down beside her. "Mom, are you okay?" I ask.

No answer.

I shake her, "Mom!"

She opens her eyes and snarls, "What do you want?"

"I want to see if you're okay," I answer politely. (I know she isn't.)

That's the wrong thing to say. She looks at me and her right eye twitches—the tell-tale sign she is drunk. "How could I be fine?" she asks. "I have a fat fucking husband that doesn't love me, and I'm stuck in this hell where I just get beat… be…" Her voice trails off as she stares off into the distance.

I shake my head in disbelief. Aside from her vulgarity, my mom is a compulsive liar when she drinks. In her mind, everybody has wronged her.

"What is that stupid face?" she growls at me. "You're so fucking ugly. You're lucky Taylor—"

"Stop! Do not say another word!" I demand.

"What? I wasn't going to say anything bad," she lies.

"I don't care," I respond. "Keep my girlfriend's name out of your mouth."

I have a short temper when she drinks, but even shorter when she gets under my skin. It took me a while to let any girls near the house. My closest friends knew our family secret, but I tried keeping it hidden from the rest of the world. As petty as it may seem, I couldn't shake the feeling that my mom's alcoholism reflected poorly on me, so I tried to keep girls away, until Taylor.

Raised family-oriented, she instantly wanted to spend time getting to know us, and it didn't take long for her to learn our secret. It didn't matter to her like I thought it would. She remained just as loving to all of us, and in a short period of time, she was family. Everybody loves her, especially my mom. Nevertheless, I don't like my mom interacting with Taylor when she is drunk. Despite what she knows, I don't want to subject my girlfriend to the horrors our family endures. Every day I see my mom wreak havoc and every day I am heart-broken. I continue to hold on to the feeling that we will break through to her, and she constantly lets me down.

I take a deep breath. It is too early in the morning to let her get to me this way. More calmly, I ask her, "Why, Mom? Why must you continue to do this to us?"

Never ready to talk about her alcoholism, sober or drunk, my mom completely changes the subject. Staring into my eyes, she asks, "Do you understand what happened to me? DO YOU?"

"No, Mom, what is it this time?" I respond.

She pops up in bed and starts screaming, "I WAS RAPED! I WAS RAPED! I WAS RAPED!" She won't stop screaming it. I get up from the bed and walk out the door, slamming it behind me. The family picture falls to the floor and breaks. I've just awakened a demon, and we are in for a day of hell.

Two

Under the Bridge

Throughout our childhood, our mom told us little about what it was like for her growing up. We asked, but received only bits and pieces. As her alcoholism and depression grew, we learned more of her truth. Our dad confirmed most of it, but some she still held inside. What I do know paints a darker picture of the woman my mom became.

Diane was born the oldest of five daughters to teenage parents, Bruce and Ann, shortly after their high school graduation. With little money and work experience, her high school sweetheart parents set off to make a life for their baby daughter. Unfortunately, times were tough, and before long, they had two baby daughters and little money to support them.

Bruce started a low-level position in a medical lab to make ends meet. Confident and passionate, he quickly moved up the ranks in the business, working long hard hours to ensure his continued advancement. It paid off.

Before they reached their thirties, Bruce and Ann had five daughters, a single-family home, and a steady income.

While Bruce spent most of his time working, Ann focused on raising the girls into proper young ladies, well-respected young women, and suitable future wives. Ann was headstrong and commanding. Her family abided by her rules, and if they didn't, there would be consequences. Ann also enjoyed her wine, and according to my mom, sometimes too much. She always called her parents "old school." Her mom believed that a woman's place was in the home and wanted to raise her daughters the "right way." As a result, Ann was tough on them. Whether it was dance competitions or training in proper etiquette, she expected perfection. If any of them failed her, she had a tendency to put them in their place... and my mom seemed to fail her a lot.

Diane always set out to please her mother, but that rarely happened. Instead, she would be crushed when Ann didn't see the effort she had put into her schoolwork, dance, field hockey, or any of the numerous jobs she took on to help pay the family bills. She succeeded in many of the things she tried; unfortunately for her, none of that success seemed to please her mother. Nothing she did was what Ann wanted for her oldest daughter, and as a result, Ann greeted many of Diane's achievements with negativity. My mom recounted the following story of when she was accepted into Ryder University:

"Mom, mom! I just received my acceptance letter from Ryder. I'm going to college!" she exclaimed.

"That's great, but how do you think you are going to pay for that?" Ann responded. "We don't have the money to put you through college. Where are you going to live? If you expect it to be at home, you'll have to pay rent."

"I'll pay for it all on my own. I don't need your help. I'm going for business and I'll work for a big company," Diane answered optimistically.

This was all we heard about our mother's childhood: small vignettes like these we tried to piece together into stories. They all started the same: my mother would take a deep breath and say, "My childhood was tough… it wasn't easy for us girls."

Each time, she would stare off into the distance for a few seconds before she told her story, and every story ended the same: "But we made do. We girls persevered and now look at us!"

There was always a sense of pride at the end. My mom took the role of the oldest sibling seriously and saw herself as a matriarch to her younger sisters. She set out to protect them, and when her mother wasn't there for them, she would act as their support system.

Until my mom started abusing alcohol, I had a completely different image of her childhood.

My grandfather, Bruce, was always a fun-loving family-oriented patriarch, adoring all sixteen of his grandchildren and willing to do anything for us. In his youth, he wasn't very different. But long, hard hours at work often ran him down, and my mom said he had a tendency to be short-tempered.

As a child, I saw my grandma, Ann, as loving, sweet, and caring, and I loved spending time with her. The only hint of strictness I experienced was when she'd yell, "Take your shoes off!" when we'd first walk into the house.

With age though, I would come to learn that Ann hadn't always been so nice, and even when I was young, I could sense a bit of fear whenever my mom talked to her. There was animosity between them that had never cleared up, and much of it started when, at seventeen, Diane experienced every girl's greatest fear.

TICK, TICK, TICK. Normally the ticking of the grandfather clock was just background noise, but on this day, it was the only sound Ann could hear. She could tell. Something was wrong.

RIIIIING! The noise of the phone made her jump. Her palms began sweating, and a sense of dread hung over her that she couldn't shake. Nervously, she answered, "Hello?"

A strange man's voice was on the other end of the line. "Your daughter has been hurt..." he said.

Just then, her youngest daughter, Danielle, walked into the kitchen and could see that something was wrong. "Mom, are you okay?"

BANG! Ann dropped the phone. She saw her other daughters join their sister who was speaking to her from across the room, but all Ann could hear was a loud buzzing in her ear. Stunned and discombobulated, she counted her children, "One... two... three... four."

Only four girls stood in front of her, so it must be true. Her instincts had been right:

She looked at the girls and exclaimed, "We have to go, NOW!"

"Ma'am, could you tell us what happened in as much detail as you remember?" the cops asked Diane.

"I can try," Diane responded, thankful that her mother hadn't yet arrived at the hospital. This would be the only time she would tell the full story. The rest of us would only receive bits and pieces.

"It was about three in the afternoon and I was taking a shortcut home through the woods. I've taken this same path every day since I was a girl, and I usually don't see anybody else. This time, I noticed a man following behind me. He was dressed normally and had nothing suspicious about him. He wore a tee-shirt tucked into a pair of blue jeans and looked like he was in his twenties, with big blue eyes. Somehow, he made me nervous. When he turned into the woods, my heart sank.

"'Miss, miss!' he called out. I gave him the benefit of the doubt because he looked harmless. I stopped and walked in his direction.

"Then, he asked, 'What is a pretty girl doing walking around these woods all alone?'

"I smiled nervously and said, 'I'm just walking home.' Scared, I told him I had to get going and started walking away swiftly.

"His smile dropped and he changed his tone.

'Why don't you stick around? I want to get to know you,' he demanded.

"Now I was sure he meant harm, so I turned around and tried to run. I'm a track runner, but I still wasn't quick enough. The man grabbed me from behind. I started scratching at his arms and hit him hard enough that it caused him to let me go.

"I started to run, but my feet gave out on me, and I fell to the ground. My arms flailed as I tried to get back to my feet.

"I felt the pressure of his knee against my back. Then I was face down in the dirt with him on top of me.

"'I wouldn't move if I were you,' he snickered as he put his knife against my throat.

"I started to scream, 'HELP, HELP ME! HELP ME!' But we were in these secluded woods, so...

"'Shut up!' He yelled. 'Shut the fuck up or I'll fucking kill you!'

"I was breathing heavily, but I stopped screaming. Tears poured down my face. In my head, I kept asking myself, Why me? Finally, it slipped out and I asked the question aloud.

"'The way you look,' he said. 'You were asking for this and you will enjoy it,' he sneered.

"With a knife against my throat, he raped me in the middle of the day right on the path I've taken a thousand times...I've never felt so helpless...The worst part was that he didn't feel any remorse."

The cops took down her story and went on their way, leaving my mom crying, broken, and feeling lost. After some tests and a check-up with the doctors, her family came into the room.

"Are you okay, Diane?" her mother asked, already aware of what had happened.

Diane just shook her head yes but started to cry. Ann held her daughter in her arms for a moment. "It will be fine," she said.

A few days later, like a switch, her compassion turned to disgust. "How could you let this happen to you?" she scolded at her defeated daughter.

"Mom, I couldn't help it!" Diane cried.

"I beg to differ. You've disgraced us. I can't even look at you. How could you do this to us? Do you understand how it's going to look to others?" Ann angrily accused.

"Mom, stop it!" Danielle yelled.

"I suggest you give your grandparents a call," Ann said. "It would be best for all of us if you live with them for a while."

So, after being raped, Diane was kicked out of her house and forced to move in with her grandparents. This was just days before the start of her senior year of high school.

THREE

Pray

Have you ever wanted to punch you own mother in the face? I have.

Mind you, I was never a fighter. My fighting career began and ended with a tussle between my friend and I when we were in grade school. Just like happens to everyone, he got under my skin, and I responded.

My dad was the fighter. His natural instinct was to fight. He glorified stories of settling scores by beating other guys to a pulp. My mom, though, often tried to practice empathy. When dealing with conflict. She tried to put herself in the other person's shoes.

So, after that fight in grade school, I saw two distinct paths for when I was overcome with anger. I could either use my fists, or I could try to see the world from the other person's perspective, just like my mom had taught me.

I chose the latter.

"Elliot, your fat pig, get your mother out of my house!" Diane yells down the stairs.

Angie bursts through her bedroom door. "Mom, what are you talking about?" she asks with an angry and confused look on her face from my mom's wailing waking her up.

"I'm not talking to you, I'm talking to your father," Diane slurs.

"No, you are yelling about Grandma Palma to Dad and he isn't even here!" Angie yells. Ang has her own short temper, but it's especially short when my mom appears drunk.

"Where is he this time? Is he cheating on me again?" Diane asks sarcastically. "Tell him to get his mother out of my house. She's not my problem!"

After just being woken up, Angie is already out of patience. "One, Dad is at work… something you know nothing about. Two, Grandma Palma does everything for us. She is more of a mom than you'll ever be, so do not talk about her like that!"

"She is not my mother! I want her OUT OF THIS HOUSE! She is NOT my responsibility!" Diane repeats.

Across the hall, my sisters' shared bedroom door swings open again, and Aubrey storms in. "What's wrong?" she asks. "It's still morning and I'm trying to sleep."

My mom suddenly turns innocent. "I just want to know where your father is, that's it."

"HE'S AT WORK," Aubrey answers.

Finally, I grow tired of the banter, "Mom, are you drunk?" I ask.

When asked such a question, my mom's response will always go one of two ways: denial mixed with remorse or lashing out. This was not meant to be a quiet day.

"No, I am not drunk, Anthony. Maybe we should call the cops and have them test you!" she responds.

I don't raise my voice; instead, I try to reason with her. "Mom, Grandma is downstairs, and we don't want to cause a scene. Please give us the alcohol and get some rest."

"I DO NOT HAVE ANY ALCOHOL. I AM NOT DRUNK!" she screams. "Check my purse."

Diane dumps her entire purse out on her bed and starts throwing all of the contents at the wall. The keys to her car just miss Angie's head and put a small ding in the drywall.

I turn to my sisters. "We better call Dad because this is going to be ugly. Stand by the door and make sure she doesn't go anywhere near Grandma."

I shut the door behind me and instantly dial my dad. With him being the general manager of his company, I understand the magnitude of asking him to leave work, but I have no other choice.

"Anthony, what's up?" he answers. "I'm in a conference call and can't talk."

"Dad, it's an emergency," I say.

"Mom?" he asks, but he already knows the answer.

"Yeah, she's drunk already and she's picking a fight with Grandma. We don't know what to do."

"She's been texting me nonsense all morning, but I couldn't believe she would be drunk this early with everyone there. Ugh... I'll come home immediately."

Before he hangs up, I hear him yell, "You have to be fucking kidding me!"

This won't end well.

I hang up with my dad and send Angie down with Grandma Palma so everything seems normal. Then I direct Aubrey to watch my mom as I quietly pack my grandma's bags.

Aubrey watches out of my parents' bedroom window, and ten minutes later sees my dad coming towards the door. She quickly texts me, "Dad's home." I run upstairs to check on my mom, and she is still throwing stuff all over the room. All of the contents from the top of my dad's dresser are already on the floor. The room looks like a tornado hit it.

My dad walks in the front door and straight at my grandma. "Diane is acting up, Mom," he whispers. "We have to get going." My grandma understands the severity of the situation and hastily gathers her bags.

"Angie, get Grandma's things and walk her out to the car," my dad directs. I walk downstairs to greet him, but he turns to me and gives me the same instructions. "Make it quick," he says. I can see it in his eyes. He is going to confront the monster.

Angie and I load my dad's car with my grandma's bags. I send Angie inside to check on our mom while I wait with my grandma in the front of the house.

My grandma turns to me and says, "You know, this is the fourth time your mom threw me out of the house."

I didn't know, and now I feel completely defeated. At eighty-eight years old and not able get around as easily, Grandma Palma's visits are few and far between. How devastating for her time with us to be constantly cut short.

"Your mother even went as far as locking me out of the house in the middle of the winter," she continues. "You kids were young so you wouldn't remember. I knocked and knocked, but nobody answered, so I was forced to sleep in the car. At least the other times I could go home or sleep in a hotel. For as long as I live, I'll never forgive what she has done, but I remain civil. Your mom has a disease and needs help."

My eyes start to well up with tears and I respond with the only words I can muster, "I'm so sorry, Grandma."

"Listen, Anthony, this is not your fault. You all try to get her help but she refuses. I just don't understand how things could be so bad in her life to cause her to act like this. You know, I lived in a one-room apartment with six siblings through the Depression, lost my mom as a child, experienced the deaths of my brothers and sisters, lost my husband, and buried my own son, yet I don't carry that burden around with me. But your mom...I fear she doesn't have much time left...." At that, my grandma's voice trails off.

She doesn't deserve this, I think as I hug her. Then I tell her I'm going to check on my dad. I have a feeling things have already gotten ugly.

I open the front door and immediately hear my mom yelling, "Fuck you, Aubrey! FUCK YOU!"

I run up the stairs to see what prompted Diane to curse out her own daughter. Before I can get up the stairs, she continues, "Fuck you! You're a slut, and I'm ashamed you're my daughter!"

I stop in place. Regardless of what my mom has said in the past, this is an all-time low.

I find my dad holding Aubrey back from her as Diane continues to berate her.

"What the fuck do you think you are going to do, slut?" she sarcastically asks, making all of our blood boil.

Even my father's strength can't hold Aubrey's anger.

WHACK! Aubrey punches our mom square in the nose, sending her falling back on the bed with blood pouring down her face. Tears run down her eyes and she's in shock.

Aubrey turns around and looks at me, defeated. She is crying and shaking—clearly pushed past her breaking point. I hug her and tell her not to listen, but I know it isn't enough to heal the pain my little sister is feeling at the moment.

From behind us, Angie cries, "How could you do this to us! You are supposed to be our mother!"

Elliot stares at his wife in disbelief, shaking his head. "How could you do this to your own children?! These are our children!"

"You didn't even want them," Diane lies. "All three of them are fucking mistakes and you know it."

"No, I don't know that. We both wanted our kids and we love them. You have to stop this. You are tearing this family apart!"

With all of her children crying in front of her, Diane responds to the situation the only way she knows how, attacking my dad where it hurts most: "Fuck you, Elliot. You aren't half the man your brother was, and you never will be."

Before I have the chance to intervene, my dad starts towards my mom. There is no turning back from what she has just said. My dad grabs both of her arms. She tries to scratch and kick, but she can't break his grip.

"Dad, DAD! Let go of Mom!" Aubrey yells.

Blind with anger, he pushes Aubrey off of him and she falls to the ground. With his eyes locked on my mom, he yells through gritted teeth, "SNAP OUT OF IT! SNAP THE FUCK OUT OF IT! THE KIDS NEED THEIR MOM, AND I NEED MY WIFE!"

"Ha! How could I ever love a fat fuck like you?" Diane snarls with a cheap grin. Then, she spits in my dad's face. "That is what I think of you, Elliot."

I immediately run towards my dad, who has a murderous look on his face.

"Anthony, I can't take this anymore!" he screams at the top of his lungs.

"Back up, Dad!" I implore him. "Turn around and look at your children. Do it for us."

My dad lets go of my mom, turns around, and hugs his daughters. Then, without saying a word, he starts down the stairs and towards the front door.

"Where is he going?" Aubrey asks.

"He's leaving us," Angie angrily answers.

I look out of my parent's bedroom window and see tears running down my dad's face as he walks down our long driveway towards his car. He's not intentionally leaving us alone. He just doesn't want us seeing him so defeated.

"He needs to take Grandma home," I try to reassure my sisters.

My mom regains her temper and responds, "Fuck you, Anthony. You're a piece of shit."

I'm baffled. "What did I do, Mom? I tried helping you."

"Help? You do nothing but hurt me! You made your father leave me…you are a piece of shit, and I want you out of my house!"

I ignore her and turn towards my sisters. "Let's leave her alone for a while. She's just going to hurt us more if we stay."

We leave the room and I slam the door again, this time permanently breaking the frame. From the outside, we hear her wailing, "Why won't he love me? Why do they do this to me?"

Out of all the pain and trouble she already caused, the only part of the morning my mom remembers is my dad leaving. She needs help.

When I step outside, I see a few neighbors gathered out front, including former friends of my mom. They are talking and pointing at our house. Still angry, I decide to confront them.

As I start towards them, a couple of the neighbors walk away. Only two remain: family friends.

"How is your mom?" they ask—a typical question and they already know the answer.

I answer anyway. "She caused a scene while my grandma was here, so my dad had to take my grandma home so it didn't get worse."

They both shake their heads. "Have you gotten her help?" one asks. "Because she needs it."

Questions like that make me want to explode, but I keep my composure, "Yes, we tried confronting the situation multiple times as a family and the cops were involved before…I'm sure you noticed."

They nod their heads, yes, but it's obvious they only want to put their two cents in.

"Well, my friend's brother had a problem with alcoholism and he went to a rehabilitation center for thirty days," one says. "He was cured after that. Why don't you try that? Have you thought about it yet? She needs it."

Without giving me a chance to answer, the other woman chimes in, "The cops can't do anything in this state, so constantly calling them is just a waste of time.

Why don't you just take her keys from her and take all of the alcohol out of your house? She can't drink if she can't get to any alcohol."

I have an answer for every one of their condescending questions. We did try rehab, but it was days before Christmas and our hearts made our decisions for us. We've tried interventions with our family, but they only buy us a week or two maximum before she starts drinking again. We call the cops because we feel helpless and hopeless, regardless of whether or not they can directly help us. We would take her keys from her if we didn't so desperately need the little money she makes from her part-time job. Even so, she has enough friends that don't know the severity of her problem, and they would get her alcohol.

Babysitting your own mother all hours of the day while trying to balance schoolwork, socializing, and the pressures of looking after your siblings is tough. Every day I open the front door to my house hoping the intervention, the cop visit, the argument, or the fight from the day before might help her realize she has a problem, and every day I am let down. As long as she is breathing, each one of us is fighting to help her overcome her disease, so condescending questions based on prejudice don't do us any good.

I bite my tongue and avoid unnecessarily explaining myself any further. I simply end the conversation, "We'll try our best to incorporate any and all ways to get my mom help. Thank you for your concern, but we have to try and figure this problem out as a family. I'll come knocking if my sisters and I need you."

They smile half-heartedly and walk away.

Just as I cross the street, I hear a high-pitched scream coming from my parent's bedroom. It is unlike anything

I've heard before. Panicked, I run up the stairs and into my house. I hear the same noise again. It's Angie.

"What's wrong?!" I yell, running up the stairs.

Angie stands in the doorway with tears running down her face. She is pointing at the other side of the room hyperventilating. Through her sobs, I can barely make out, "Mom... wants to...kill... herself..."

In the middle of the room stands my mom with a knife in her left hand. Blood drips from the top of the blade and her chest is stained with red.

FOUR

Breaking Down

Knock, Knock, Knock! "Mom? Are you in there?" I asked.

"WHY? WHY DID THIS HAPPEN? SHE'S TOO YOUNG!" she wailed through the door.

"Mommy, it's Anthony. Can I come in?"

The door swung open and my mom stood in front of me. Streaks of makeup ran down her face and her eyes were red. She had been crying. I had never seen her look so distraught.

"Are you okay?" I asked anxiously.

"I'll be fine, hon," she responded, her cheeks wet with tears. "Sit down, I have to tell you something important."

Concerned, I sat down on her bed.

My mom continued, "Mom-Mom has been sick for quite a while. You might have noticed her in bed a lot recently. She did a good job of hiding her illness for a while, but ...she was in a lot of pain..." My mom's voice trailed off, her eyes squinted, and she squeezed my hand.

After a short pause, she spoke softer through tears, "She held on to see her beautiful grandchildren… to see you. I'm sorry, Anthony, but Mom-Mom is gone."

My eyes started to water. Looking at me ever so lovingly, my mom wiped my tears away with her sleeve and tried to comfort me. "Don't worry," she said. "She's in a better place and isn't in any more pain."

At 63, after a ten-year battle with cancer, Grandma Ann had passed away.

I sat on the bed dumbfounded. At ten, death was still an abstract concept, but I understood one part of it: my mom would no longer be able to talk to, hug, or spend holidays with her mom. She would no longer be able to find comfort in her mom's words or tell her mom she loved her.

I thought about my mom and how I'd feel if she was suddenly taken away from me, and I started to cry, mostly because I felt lucky she was still there. My mom picked me up and squeezed me tight. "You have to promise me one thing," she said as she cried.

Resting my head against her chest, I nodded yes.

"No matter how mad you are at me," she continued, "you will always tell me how much you love me."

I looked up at her, wondering why she was telling me this.

"Listen," she reassured me, "I'm not going anywhere, but you never know what can happen. Just remember, Mommy will always love you. Show me how much."

I smiled and stretched my arms out to my side to show her.

After Grandma Ann passed, holidays felt different because we were now missing our matriarch, but we used the time to bond over the loving memories of our grandma. My mom shared her own fond stories, but something was different. She seemed more reserved. On the one-year anniversary of her mother's death, I learned why:

"No, you are NOT fit to drive. Let me pay the bill and I will take us all home," my dad angrily whispered to my mom at our table at the local pizzeria.

"Elliot, I'm leaving; I WANT TO LEAVE NOW!" Diane yelled.

All eyes in the dining room were on us, including the owners and some family friends, whose son I played baseball with. Embarrassed, I put my head down and did not look up from the table.

"Diane, the waitress will be back in a minute. Please wait and I'll take us home," my dad pleaded. He then got up to find the owners so he could pay at the counter.

As my dad left the dining room, Diane screamed, "Fuck you, Elliot!" Then she turned to my sisters and I. "We're leaving, RIGHT NOW!"

Scared and confused, I asked, "Shouldn't we wait for dad to come back?"

She snapped back, "If you want to wait, then wait. I DON'T need you because I have my daughters. Screw you, Anthony."

She got up, picked up Angie and led Aubrey toward the door, leaving me at the table.

"Daddy! DADDY!" Angie wailed as she was carried out the front door.

Ignoring the watchful eyes, I ran after them. When I got outside, my mom and sisters were already in the car while my dad stood outside pleading to her through the driver-side window, "You can leave, but give me my daughters. THEY ARE ONLY BABIES!"

Too late. Our black SUV screeched away. Stunned, my dad and I waited outside until we could no longer hear the faint sounds of my sisters crying.

"Dad, where did Mom go?" I asked as we walked through the parking lot of the pizzeria.

"She went home, buddy. Mom was in a rush, so we decided she was going to leave a little early. I think it's a good thing because you and I will get to spend some time together. The walk will do us good anyway. Baseball season is right around the corner!" He grabbed my hand and with a forced smile said, "Let's get going, Ant. We'll be home before you know it."

Normally a mile wouldn't seem so far, but it was winter. Wind whipped our faces as we trudged through the few inches of freshly fallen snow. Only conversations about school, baseball, and the Mets shielded us from the cold. Little did I know, these trivial conversations would be my dad and I's saving grace for years to come.

After an hour that felt like an eternity, we reached our house. We both let out a sigh of relief, but our troubles did not end there. When my dad shook the doorknob, we both knew it was locked, and since Diane had driven home, she had the keys. "You have to be fucking kidding me," my dad muttered under his breath.

Scared of getting him angrier, I hustled to the garage door and put in the code to open it. I did not want to see what would happen if we couldn't get in the house. It didn't work. Diane had disabled the power to the garage to keep us from getting inside.

My dad looked over at me, "Any luck?" I just shook my head. His usual happy glow faded and his eyebrows furrowed. He pounded on the front door and screamed until his hand couldn't take any more.

I ran around the house to our backyard. My gloveless hands felt frozen stiff, but I still managed to hoist myself over our fence against the cold wind. My heart pounded in my chest. I could not let my dad down. I closed my eyes as I tried to open the back door. Locked. We had exhausted all options. Only my mom could let us in now.

I looked into the dark house. No movement. My eyes fixed on my reflection in the glass door. There I stood freezing, crying, and confused because my own mother had locked me out of my house.

Scared of how he'd react, I told my dad the bad news. "Why would Mom lock us out?" I asked. "Does she not love us?"

My dad mustered the only bit of civility he had left. "You know she loves you, Ant. Your mother had a tough year. She doesn't mean to hurt you. It's late. Maybe she fell asleep, okay?"

I nodded my head in agreement.

"Now dry those tears off before they freeze on your face. I have a game for us," he said with a smile. "We'll make snowballs and throw them at my bedroom wall. The person who wakes Mom up is the winner."

Excited, I helped my dad make a pile of snowballs, and we started hurling them at our house. This is awesome! I thought to myself.

After twenty minutes and countless snowballs, our hands were purple. With my last throw, the light to the bedroom flickered on.

"I won!" I yelled as I smiled at my dad. He didn't respond. Instead, his eyes remained focused on his bedroom window where my mom's familiar shadow now glared down at us.

He gave up on remaining quiet for the neighbors and yelled, "Let us the fuck in, Diane! Diane! LET US IN!"

The light turned off.

We gave up. After waking a neighbor, my dad found me a bed for the night, and he resorted to sleeping in his unlocked car. Without the keys or a blanket, he found little relief from the cold.

That would be the last time we left the house without planning contingencies for getting back in. For most of my childhood, my mom's alcoholism occurred in isolated incidents like these. Unfortunately, when it was bad, it was BAD.

My baseball games were a crapshoot. One game she'd be my number one fan, but the next, she'd be hurling insults at me from the sidelines. Luckily, due to her tendency to pass out early, my mom missed a majority of my games. When she did make it drunk, she would yell at my dad in front of my teammates and their parents. From the field, I'd hear, "Fuck you, Elliot!" My dad would often try to send her home to avoid a scene, but it always made matters worse.

My dad was no angel either. When I had a bad game, he would berate me in front of my teammates, worse than my mom when she was drunk. His dream was for me to be the next David Wright, so when I wasn't playing like a professional, he let me know it.

"Stop embarrassing yourself and get off the field!" he would shout from the bleachers. The pressure to play well and please my dad constantly hung over my head.

When sober, my mom was my rock. She kept my head up when my dad went on one of his tirades. She'd pull me aside after a game, give me a kiss on the top of my head, and comfort me saying, "To me, you are the best baseball player no matter how you play."

And every time, she would finish with, "Can't is not in our vocabulary. You CAN do it. Stay positive, Anthony. Good things will happen."

That bit of encouragement kept me positive through many of the tribulations of my childhood.

Unfortunately, as I got older, it became progressively rare to see my mom at my baseball games, and at a time when I needed her most, I felt more and more alone. Diane's disease was progressing. Her addiction was growing. What once were isolated incidents evolved into daily occurrences.

My sisters and I noticed my mom's worsening drinking habits a couple years after her own mom's passing, and though we were still young, we took it upon ourselves to confront the situation while on one of our family vacations:

"Dad, dad! When are we going back to the amusement park?" Aubrey asked while we were vacationing at Universal Studios – Florida. As children, we were excited about the rides, but our parents were not.

"Aubrey, later," my dad answered.

"Why can't we go now?" I chimed in. At twelve, I didn't fully understand why we couldn't keep going.

My dad quickly barked back, "Anthony, your mother and I work hard. We get one week off a year, and we will spend it how we want! We want to have a few drinks, so that's what we're doing. We'll go later."

Disappointed, I walked away. For the first time, I realized that alcohol wasn't just "for fun." It was an escape—an outlet for when they were stressed.

Later that night, we took the ferry back to the amusement park.

"Elliot, move over. This seat is wet," my mom said to my dad.

"You get up and move!" My dad snapped back. The animosity in that sentence left my sisters and me uneasy. We had missed an earlier scuffle, and whatever it had been about, it felt like it would get worse.

For the entire twenty-minute ferry ride, my parents sat next to each other, never making eye contact. My aunt and uncle had had more than a few beers themselves prior to leaving the hotel, but they still could tell trouble was brewing.

Once the ferry docked, I felt a sense of relief. But as we approached the front gate, my mom asked, "Elliot, you have the kids' tickets, right?"

"No? Why would I have them?" my dad responded.

"Well, how the fuck are we supposed to get in?" she chastised him. "God forbid you worry about somebody other than yourself."

My dad scrunched up his face and clenched his fists. I cringed. My parents were about to have one of their infamous screaming matches right in front of the gate of the amusement park. I looked over at my sisters. Only five, Angie dug her head into my mom's leg as if to brace for impact, while Aubrey, only a few years older, started to walk away from our family altogether.

Just as my dad opened his mouth to let loose, my aunt stepped in, "Elliot, I have their tickets," she said meekly.

We all let out a brief sigh of relief. She had saved us from embarrassment, but I still didn't feel at ease. My dad shot my mom a glare that made it clear the problem was not resolved. You could cut the tension with a knife.

As we entered the park, I hesitantly walked behind the group, nervous that another shouting match would occur. My dad noticed me and pulled me by my hand to catch me up with the rest of our family. He quickly let go and looked down at me, "Why are your hands so clammy?" he asked. Before I could answer, he had another question, "This is where you wanted to go, right?"

It was, but not now...not like this. This was our first family vacation out of the Northeast, the result of six months of planning, a year's worth of savings, and the most exciting Christmas gift I had ever received, but that amusement park on that night was the last place in the world I wanted to be. I felt a terrible sense of foreboding about the night ahead, but I did not want to get my dad any more agitated by expressing my apprehension, so I lied.

"I'm really excited, Dad... Thank you," I answered.

"You better be," he responded as he dragged me along.

"Elliot, Elliot! Hold up!" My aunt called from behind us as my Dad continued to drag me in front of the group. "Let's jump on this first ride. We haven't tried it yet."

"Okay, that's a good idea," my dad agreed. His face mellowed and I let out another short sigh of relief. "I'm going to stop by a stand for a drink," he added. "Does anyone want one?"

"Yes, I'll have one!" my mom answered excitedly.

My parents walked over to the stand together, hand-in-hand. All seemed fine again. From a distance, we saw them laughing and smiling. It seemed that the cure for their bitterness was more alcohol, but it was also a recipe for disaster.

A few minutes later, we were in line for the ride. "Are you sure the kids can handle this," my dad joked. "I heard it's scary," he added, nudging my arm.

My parents finished their drinks and we all jumped on the ride. But during the ride, my sisters and I got separated from the group, and afterward, we followed the path towards the exit where everyone found one another, except for my parents. My uncle walked around to see if he could spot them. That's when we heard a familiar voice in the distance.

"Elliot, get me another drink!" Diane wailed.

"Diane, you're done. I'm not getting you shit after what you just said to me," he replied.

She continued, "Who are you to cut me off? Get me a fucking drink!"

People around us started to watch and listen. My aunt took notice and stepped in, "Diane, I'll get you a drink."

But Diane had her mind made up. With a menacing stare, she dumped the remains of her drink on my dad's head. It seemed as though everyone in the amusement park had their eyes on him now. In an instant, Diane grabbed my sisters' hands and snarled, "You finish that one. I'll grab my own fucking drink."

We yelled for her to come back, but it was drowned out by a loud park announcement, and my mom and sisters disappeared into the crowd.

Fed up, my dad threw his hands in the air. "Fuck this, I'm leaving too," he said.

My eyes started to well up, but before I could get too upset, my uncle mussed my hair and said, "C'mon buddy, let's head back. Your parents will be waiting."

I knew he meant well, but I felt alone and confused. In a matter of minutes, both my parents had left me in an amusement park without thinking twice of it.

The fifteen-minute ferry ride felt like it took hours as I nervously anticipated the situation I was walking into at the hotel. We took the elevator up to our floor and scenarios ran through my head of what I was going to find. I pictured my dad punching holes through the door to our room to break it open or my mom throwing his clothes into the hallway while the other guests judged from a distance.

I watched the elevator go up each floor: ONE... TWO... THREE... FOUR. We stopped and the door opened. I was too nervous, so I shut my eyes. To my surprise, I didn't hear a sound. I expected cursing, loud bangs, and slamming doors; at least that would be familiar. The peace and quiet put me more on edge than I was before.

My uncle held his hand against the elevator door to keep it open. "Anthony, head down to your room and check the door. If it's open, we'll feel safe leaving you for the night. Come right back here if you have ANY problems. We'll take you in if need be," my uncle assured me.

I walked down the hall to our room and put my ear against the door, but there was no sound. I tried the handle and found it was unlocked, so I called down the hall to my aunt and uncle to let them know.

My aunt responded, "If you need anything, don't hesitate to knock."

I nodded as the elevator doors closed. Again, I let out a sigh and assumed it was the end of a terrible night. Once again, I was wrong. I pushed the door open, but it stopped halfway. Something was blocking it. Fed up and determined to get into the room, I planted my feet and used my body to heave it open. No matter how hard I tried, I could not get in. I looked through the crack and saw a large chair pressed against the door. It was too heavy for me to move alone.

BANG, BANG, BANG. I knocked on the door and continued to push. "It's Anthony, could someone let me in?" I asked in a whisper. The last thing I wanted right now was to bring any more attention to this embarrassing situation.

Footsteps came in my direction. Rather than a warm hello, I was welcomed with the door slamming closed in my face. Then, I heard my mom put the bolt lock on the door and she whispered back, "Find somewhere else to sleep tonight."

With my back against the door, I sunk to the floor, defeated. I slumped to the elevator, took it back to the lobby and walked outside. I wandered aimlessly around the perimeter of the hotel waiting for life to point me in the right direction.

The waves of the bay splashed along the side of the walkway as a bright light blinded me for a few seconds. The ferry was pulling up to the hotel and docking to take one last group to the amusement park. I figured that surrounded by people was the best place to feel alone.

As I headed towards the boat, I was flooded with feelings of helplessness, and somehow an image of a former classmate of mine flashed in my mind.

Two years prior I had been shocked to learn she had died at the age of twelve from an unknown heart condition. I had been overcome with grief knowing that a girl I had grown up with had passed away so unexpectedly. When I heard the news, I had paced up and down the hallway of my school trying to comprehend the situation. No matter how hard I tried, I couldn't get past the finality of her death. I had experienced loss before, but she had been my age and had so much more life to live. The future seemed so bleak knowing that such realities were totally out of my control. Such was the case with my mom. Nothing I did was helping her to get better, and I was running out of options.

As I approached the entrance to the boat, I thought to myself, I don't know how I'd be able to manage losing her like I lost Julia.

"Are you alone?" the captain asked.

Scared he wouldn't let me on without a parent, I lied, "I'm meeting my dad at the park."

He nodded as if that answer was sufficient. With a southern drawl and a smile, he said, "I'll get you to your pops in a jiffy. You sit back and enjoy the ride… the bay is beautiful tonight."

It was. A cool breeze kissed my face as the boat started to move. The moon's reflection glistened off the water and drew me into self-reflection. I tried to understand what I did to cause my parents to leave me behind. I felt alone and unwanted like a facedown penny on the sidewalk waiting for someone to pick it up.

Just when I needed it most, a familiar voice asked, "Is this seat taken?"

I nodded my head as my uncle sat beside me. "How did you find me?"

"I just had a feeling you could use some company," he answered with a smile. "What brings you out here alone?"

"My parents… as usual. They like alcohol more than they like us," I muttered.

"No, that's not true. They love you and your sisters," he assured me.

After being left behind on vacation and locked out of my room, I did not want to hear any more excuses for them. Tears rolled down my face as I shook my head. "It is true," I snapped. "How could they love us if they always choose to drink instead of being our parents?"

My uncle put his hand on my shoulders and repeated, "Your parents love you and your sisters. They work very hard during the week, and alcohol helps them relax."

I looked at my uncle, puzzled, so he continued, "Alcohol helps both me and your parents relax during the weekends. If just for a moment, it helps us forget whatever problems we've had during the week. Do you understand?"

I nodded, but I still had questions. "If it is supposed to help them relax on the weekends, why do they drink during the week and get in fights?"

My uncle looked at me sternly. "Alcohol has different effects on people, and at times, makes them angry or even sad. If you don't like how they act when they drink, you should tell them. Communication is key, so they understand how you feel. Trust me, Anthony, I never did that when I was your age, and I wish I had. I lost my mom when I was just a boy and my dad drank alcohol to ease the pain. Unfortunately, he drank his 'medicine' seven days a week until I lost him too. Talk to your parents because they love you and care about you very much."

"Thank you," I said with a smile.

"Anytime, buddy. Let's head back. We've had enough adventure for one night."

When the boat docked at the park, we remained on board until it took us back to the hotel.

My aunt gave me a big hug when we walked into their hotel room. She had a bed made up for me on the floor and made sure I was comfortable before going to sleep. For a few moments, I forgot about all that had happened that night and I relaxed into sleep.

The next morning, I headed back to my hotel room. To my surprise, the door was propped open and my mom was waiting in the doorway.

"Where were you, honey?" she asked.

With my head down, I answered, "I had to sleep in someone else's room because you locked me out."

She looked at me confused, "I did not lock you out. Maybe your father did, but I would never do that to you."

My eyebrows furrowed and my lips curled. "YOU locked me out. YOU caused a big scene at the amusement park. And YOU blame everyone except for YOU!"

My mom shook her head, "I'm innocent, Anthony. I was tired so I grabbed the girls and we went to bed. That's it."

For the first time, I realized that alcohol must have some effect on memory because my mom really did not remember anything from the night before. All she could do was piece together what she could recall, and fill in the blanks with fake memories. In her mind, my dad caused her to leave the park and locked me out of the hotel room.

Before I could attempt to explain the truth, my dad walked in. Instantly, my mom stopped babbling and changed her tone. Unlike the night before, she greeted him with open arms.

"Why would I hug you after what you did to us last night?" he barked. "It was a complete embarrassment."

Not interested in hearing my parents bicker again, I snuck off to another part of the hotel room where my sisters were hiding.

Still mad, I asked my sisters, "Why didn't either of you let me in last night?"

"Mom wouldn't let us," Aubrey quickly answered. "She made us put stuff around the door so no one could get in."

I wanted to be mad at them but I couldn't. I had been on the other side of the door before myself, and there was no reason to make them feel any worse.

"Mom and dad only fight really bad when they drink alcohol," Aubrey pointed out. "We have to get them to stop."

"How could we do that?" I asked.

"We should ask them to stop because it makes their kids upset. They care about us, so it doesn't make sense for them to keep drinking if they know it makes us feel bad," she answered.

Remembering my talk with my uncle, I agreed with Aubrey. "We should have them sign a contract. That way, they can't forget our agreement and when they do drink, we can show it to them so they stop before they start to fight," I explained.

With my parents still arguing, my sisters and I wrote down all of our reasons why our parents should stop drinking. At the bottom, we left two lines for their signatures. Then we sent little Angie to disrupt them, knowing that with their youngest, they would be more inclined to listen.

"Mommy and daddy, I have something for you," Angie squeaked. Aubrey and I stood a few nervous steps behind her.

"What is this baby?" my dad asked as he reached for the contract. He motioned to my mom to come read it with him. Aubrey and I walked towards Angie and we all sat down to listen:

Dear Dad and Mom,

We are very hurt due to the amount of drinking that takes place. We understand that you like to have fun, but we are getting hurt. This isn't the first vacation that was ruined because of alcohol and we want it to stop. You guys get in fights every time you drink, and we are always stuck in the middle of it. Your kids and our family would be happy if you both stopped drinking alcohol. Please try, for us. Sign below so you can't break our contract.

Mom _____

Dad _____

Love,
Anthony, Aubrey, Angie

Both of my parents started to tear up. When he finished reading, my dad wiped away his tears and felt compelled to explain. "Your mother and I usually drink alcohol to have fun after working hard during the week. Those long hours get you guys all the things you enjoy. I'll admit, sometimes we get too carried away... How about this? Let's come to a compromise: We will add to the contract that we cannot drink during the week but can only drink during the weekends when it is mommy and daddy time."

My sisters and I huddled up. After some deliberation, we nodded our heads in agreement.

My dad smiled and assured us, "We will commit to every word of this family pact. Right, Diane?"

She nodded yes. "We both love you very much and promise that we will continue to do what it takes to make you happy. You kids are our whole lives," she professed.

They both signed on the lines, and the deal was sealed.

Part II

Purgatory

FIVE

Save Me

Drip. Drip. Drip. Blood falls slowly off of the tips of the knife onto the floor. Otherwise, the room is silent. Blood seeps too through a large slash in the middle of my mom's chest, staining her spaghetti-string top.

We are in a stand-off: my sisters and I on one side of the bedroom, and my mom on the other. Each of us is scared to make a move because, if we startle her, Diane may act drastically again. I turn to Ang, "Call the police."

"No!" my mom yells. "If you call the fucking police, I will kill myself right now!" she threatens, lifting the knife and pressing the point against the left side of her chest.

Without hesitation, Aubrey darts for her. With her right hand, she pushes my mom backwards and, with her left, pulls the knife out of Diane's grip, unknowingly by the blade, sending blood pouring down her hand.

"You are NOT killing yourself, do you hear me?!" Aubrey screams at the top of her lungs.

"Oh yes I am," Diane slurs in response. In a matter of seconds, she darts for the window and opens it. The screen is still missing from a previous suicide threat, and she climbs halfway out of her third-story window.

I jump over my parent's bed and grab her by the waist to keep her from leaping out. She kicks and screams as I safely bring her back into the bedroom, closing the window behind her.

My mom grabs me by the hands and looks at me with tears in her eyes. "Anthony, please let me die," she cries. "Please let me end this hell I'm living in. Please, for your mother," she pleads.

Instantly, I am flooded with compassion. I feel the pain in her heart, and all I want to do is help her. All my anger washes away, and I do the only thing I know how to do as her son. I hug her and pour my remaining love into her.

"Mom, you do not want to kill yourself," I assure her. "You have all you need to live for in this room," I say nodding to my sisters.

"You guys don't love me anymore," she weeps, still in my arms.

"Yes, we do! We love you, Mommy!" Aubrey exclaims as she joins in our embrace.

We all sit down on the bed to continue to calm her down. As we do so, Aubrey checks her cut to judge the severity of it. "It doesn't look deep," she whispers to me. She's wrong. It is bleeding at an alarming rate.

As my mom finally calms down, Ang walks back into the room with her phone to her ear. In all the commotion, Aubrey and I had not seen her sneak away.

"Ant, I don't know what to say to them," Angie whispers to me.

My mom pops out of bed with her eyes wide open. "Say WHAT…to WHO?" she nervously stammers.

"Give me the phone. I'll talk to them," I respond, ignoring my mom.

"TALK TO WHO?" Diane repeats louder with her lip quivering. I ignore her again so she continues, "I know who you're talking to... THE FUCKING COPS!"

"No, Mom. We just want to get someone to help you with your cut," Aubrey calmly attempts to reassure her.

She doesn't listen. Instead, she dashes towards the bedroom door. With Angie's phone in my left hand, I wrap my right arm around her waist keeping her in the room, all the while attempting to explain the situation to the emergency operator on the phone.

Our mom has a history of fleeing the house when the cops are called. If she does, there is nothing the cops can do to help, and as we have often been reminded by Pennsylvania state authorities, we cannot force her into in-patient rehab except in severe cases of mental distress. In my mind, all that has transpired should finally qualify. We can't trust her to remain alone anymore.

"Aubrey, watch Mom so she doesn't do anything stupid. DO NOT let her out of the room," I command.

I close the door and move to our backyard to avoid my mom hearing the conversation. Thank God the police dispatcher is patient with us and is still on the line.

"Sir, what is going on?" she asks.

"Sorry, ma'am, my mom is drunk and carrying on. After roughly ten years of alcoholism, she's become a danger to herself, now more than ever. We've called the cops many times before, and she's threatened to commit suicide in the past, but she really hurt herself this time," I say as if rehearsed.

"Where did she hurt herself? What did she do?"

"She cut herself with a knife in the chest."

"Is it still bleeding?"

"Yes. It's bleeding a lot, but my sisters are attempting to stop it."

"Okay. Whom am I speaking with?"

"Anthony. I'm her son."

"Alright, Anthony. I'm sending an officer and an ambulance for your mom. Keep her in sight and try to clean out the wound before they arrive."

I hang up and let out a deep breath. With all of the insanity of the day, I finally see a sliver of hope. Now that my mom took it far enough to cut herself, we may finally be able to get her the help she needs. Nevertheless, it's tough to swallow what is happening.

"Fuck," I whisper under my breath. My mom's alcoholism has caused plenty of unwanted attention to our family before, but this time may be the worst of all. I absolutely do not want to be the one to tell my dad.

I walk inside through the back door just as Angie walks in through the front door, so I ask for her to break the news to him. Begrudgingly, she agrees. But first, she asks if I saw our mom's car. Confused, I walk outside to check our mom's usual parking spot across the street. To my surprise, the car is gone.

"Fuck!" This time I don't whisper. When my mom is drunk and notices a cop car while driving, she believes that parking her car away from the house will cover the fact she's been drinking and driving. To keep from pulling Aubrey away from watching my mom, I text her to let her know I'm leaving to look for the car. Luckily, she texts back with a bit of good news: both her and my mom's hands have stopped bleeding.

With one less issue to worry about, I head out to scout the neighborhood. I calculate the amount of time I'll have to search for the car before the cops arrive: about five minutes based on previous calls. I check her usual spots without any luck. With each failed attempt, I fear the worst. After multiple incidents and car accidents, we cannot afford another. We are already eighteen thousand dollars in debt. I already expect a blow-up when my dad gets home, so I'd like to at least assure him the car is safe. Before I can find it, though, I hear a brigade of sirens headed towards my house.

"Let the show begin," I groan as I jog back to my street.

"Is this your house, son?" The officer asks.

"Yes, sir. I called about my mom."

He takes out a notepad from his shirt pocket. "Anthony, right? I'm Officer Barley."

He is a tall muscular man with brown hair fading to gray and a large mustache to match. He appears to be around 60 and carries himself like a veteran.

"Where is your mother now?" he asks.

"She's upstairs in her bedroom. Would you like to come inside?" I nervously ask.

I know my dad won't appreciate parading a team of police officers around our house in the condition it is in. Nevertheless, Officer Barley signals a short blonde female officer with the last name Cici to join us. Just as she does, two large, male EMTs hustle out of the ambulance with a medical bag.

We walk up the long flight of stairs and through the second-floor front door. To our right, we notice a bloody handprint on the railing in the entryway. Office Cici whispers something to the EMTs and we continue.

The crew stops and scans our living room. At one time, it had been classy space with a bar, dining room, and top-of-the-line entertainment system. Now, it is a symbol of how my mom's addiction has taken over our family. Clothes lie scattered around the floor, our decorative tree has toppled onto our couch, and the dining room table harbors miscellaneous broken items our mom threw at us while she was drunk.

The officers wander past our bar and notice numerous plastic, pint-sized vodka bottles. Recognizing their curiosity, I explain that my sisters found eight pints hidden around the house and dumped them out to stop our mom from drinking. They both nod as if what I explained was common.

Still assessing the house, I follow the officers into the kitchen. Immediately, all of our shoes stick to the floor and there is a strong odor. I let out an embarrassed sigh as again, I feel compelled to explain. Diagnosed with diabetes, our little Scottish Terrier needs a lot of attention. Other than two shots of insulin in her back each day, Bella needs to be let outside constantly because she has no control over the amount of water she drinks and often treats our kitchen as her toilet. As gross as the explanation is, the cops remain professional.

The rest of the kitchen is just as disgusting. Spaghetti sauce is splattered on the stove and microwave. Diane likes to cook while she is drunk, but once she leaves the room, she forgets what she was doing. As a result, half of the food we buy gets ruined. The night before, she forgot she was making pasta, so we came home to sauce that had exploded out of the pan. On top of that, the remnants of chicken teriyaki and broken glass are all over the countertops and floor from the time she threw a plate of leftover Chinese food at my dad.

Our house is in such bad condition, I apologize to everyone.

Officer Barley responds, "Son, you wouldn't believe how much worse we've seen. You live in a beautiful home. We understand the situation."

I felt slightly less embarrassed.

"Officer Barley, you better come upstairs," an EMT calls from the top of the stairs. I didn't realize it, but as we were surveying the first floor of the house, the EMTs had snuck upstairs to check on my mom. My heart sinks into a pit in my stomach. Something has happened.

We start up the stairs but stop when we see more blood. This time, it is smeared down the railing and there are a few bloody handprints on the wall.

Officer Barley stops in front of the broken door frame and looks in my direction. I nod, confirming that it too is from my mom.

We walk in to find Aubrey talking to the EMTs. But my mother isn't there.

"She tried jumping out of the window again, so I grabbed her," Aubrey explains to the EMT through tears. "She swung her fist at my face and barely missed. I pushed her and knocked her over. I tried not letting her out of the room, but she continuously called me a whore and told me she wouldn't care if I killed myself. I couldn't take it anymore, so I just let her go," she cries.

I sigh in disbelief.

Aubrey sees me and starts to cry more.

I don't blame her for letting Mom go. I just hug her.

"I-I'm sorry, Ant. I just c-c-couldn't take hearing that from mom. That was even too f-f-far for her," Aubrey sobs.

"It's okay, Aubrey. I understand. It's okay," I reassure her as I continue to hug her. We don't usually show such affection, but she's been forced to endure more abuse this morning than a person should in a lifetime. The officers and EMTs look at each other slightly stunned by the pain they are witnessing.

"We are going to find your mom and get her the help she needs," Officer Barley assures us.

Aubrey shows them a picture of my mom to help them find her. "She is skinnier than in the picture," she explains. "She doesn't eat anymore, only drinks. Her hair's a mess, her white shirt is bloody. She's in green shorts and isn't wearing any shoes."

Officer Cici steps out of the bedroom and alerts the dispatcher on a walkie-talkie. They all file back out of the front door of our house. Before they leave, they attend to Aubrey's hand.

"We should look for Mom too," I suggest to my sisters once they're all gone.

Aubrey agrees, but Ang doesn't. "I'm not looking for her," she snaps.

"Why?" I question her.

"Look at what she's done to us. I don't care if she's lost, and I don't care if she ever comes back. Diane is not my mom. She's never been a mom to me!" she yells angrily.

She's right. Being only three when my mom's addiction took over, Angie rarely experienced my mom sober. While Aubrey and I had time to develop a relationship with our mom, she never did.

"Even if we did find Mom, the cops aren't going to do anything. They're just going to wish us 'good luck' like they usually do," Ang adds bitterly.

I ignore her last statement and direct her to stay home in case our mom comes back. She agrees, and Aubrey and I walk outside to start our search.

"You know she's right. We haven't gotten help in the past, and we've called at least fifteen times over the past few years," Aubrey says. "Different officers, same situation, same results."

"I know, but I didn't want to tell Ang that. Be optimistic. I really think it will be different this time. I promise it'll be different…" My voice trails off at the end. My optimism is fading quickly.

Aubrey and I go in separate directions to cover more ground. We each carry hope, overwhelmed by doubt. Voluntarily is the only way we know that our mom can check herself into a rehab center, and in the past she has refused, whether sober or drunk. Too smart to 'act-up' around police officers, Diane hides her true self from them, and they usually just inform us they can't help do much more than calm her down.

As I wander aimlessly around the neighborhood, I think back to the awkward tour of my house and the mass amounts of vodka bottles. Just then, it dawns on me: my mom's coping mechanism when she's drunk and angry is simply more alcohol! Every time my mom drinks, she gets behind the wheel of her car and stays within a two-mile radius, only traveling to the liquor store, bar, or convenience store for cigarettes. When we do try and take her keys, she either has another set hidden or belittles us to the point where we no longer care to keep her safe. I dread another call about my mom being in a bad accident. I run back home, sprint past Angie sitting on the front steps, and check each room for my mom's purse. It's not there; neither are her keys. I head back through the front door and tell Ang my conclusion on our mom's whereabouts.

"Good, maybe she'll get pulled over or get in another accident. That's the only way she'll ever be arrested," she answers.

I look at my youngest sister, puzzled. Plenty of times in the past, I made empty threats worse than Angie's. But mine were just that: empty. "I want her to be arrested too,

Ang, but we have to make sure she's okay." Angie senses my shock at her intense animosity towards our mom. "Ant, you don't know what it's like to live here anymore since you've been at college. And now that she has her license, Aubrey isn't even here anymore. It's only me. EVERY. SINGLE. DAY. Dad and I sometimes escape the house, but it doesn't help. I just can't do it anymore. I can't take it!" she weeps.

I sigh. The pain in her voice is startling and heartbreaking. At only fourteen, my little sister spent most of her childhood longing for my mom's affection but instead received a lifetime's worth of mental abuse.

Through the sorrow in her voice, Angie asks, "Out of the ten times we called the cops on Mom so far this year, how many times has she been arrested or received help?"

"None," I admit.

"Every time we call, we're told that the cops can't force Mom into rehab and can't arrest her because 'drinking in her house isn't a crime.' We're stuck bringing all of this attention on ourselves just to watch our own mom kill herself, and I'm just not doing it anymore," Ang cries as she walks back into the house.

Just as I turn to follow her in, I spot Aubrey running down the street. "I just saw mom drive by me!" she exclaims as she runs up the front-stairs of the house.

"She must have known where her car was hidden. Which way was she going?"

Aubrey points left indicating the direction of the liquor store.

"We have to tell the cops. She could barely walk, she was so drunk. I'm afraid of what'll happen if she gets back in that car," I say.

Aubrey says she recognized a cop car parked across the street from our neighborhood, so we venture towards it. As we approach the car, we notice Officer Barley sitting behind the wheel.

"Excuse me, Officer, we have an update on my mom," I say through the open driver's side window.

"Good to hear!" he exclaims. "I'm writing up a report now. I promise we're still trying to find her so we can get her the help she needs."

"Thank you. Aubrey just saw her driving past our house in the direction of the liquor store."

"What is the make and model of the vehicle?"

"Black Kia Soul. There's a large scratch on the side of it."

Officer Barley turns away from us and picks up a walkie-talkie. "Attention to any available officers: We have an intoxicated middle-aged brunette female driving a black Kia Soul possibly heading towards the liquor store on Halloway Road. Detain her if possible."

He turns back to us and asks, "Do you happen to know the license plate?"

"JK43-7K39," Aubrey rattles off.

He thanks her and gives a few more details over the radio before turning his attention back to us.

"It may not be the best manner to do so, but if we arrest your mom for driving while intoxicated, we may be able to enter her into some programs to help her addiction. Unfortunately, she would lose her license for some time and it would be on her record," he explains.

"Sir, anything is worth it as long as we can get her help," I state. "Thank you."

Aubrey and I start to walk back home. "There's no way Mom will be able to drive by every officer in our town without getting caught, right?" she asks.

"Knowing Mom's luck, probably. But let's hope not... By the way, it was pretty impressive you could remember her license plate numbers like that," I joke.

"Ang and I memorized it so it's easier to track her car. We call the cops on her a lot when she's driving in hopes she'll be arrested. It hasn't worked yet, but maybe it will this time," Aubrey explains.

"Yeah... maybe..."

She walks inside our house to update Angie, but I feel compelled to sit outside. It's already late afternoon, and a cool breeze washes over me, giving me my first bit of relief of the day. A clear evening sky is promising me a better end to a shitty situation. As far as I'm concerned, my mom is worth fighting for.

Before I get too lost in thought, my phone rings. I assume it's my dad because we are waiting for him to check-in on the situation, but the number says 'unknown.'

"Hello..." I tentatively answer.

"Anthony, it's Officer Barley. You need to come to the elementary school immediately. We found your mom."

SIX

Every Year, Every Christmas

Our carefully constructed contract lay in the bottom of an old faded straw chest at the foot of our parents' bed long forgotten. As the years went on, our family dynamic changed entirely. Once close-knit, our family started to drift apart as my mother's alcoholism worsened and isolated incidents became daily occurrences.

"Why?" My aunt politely asked when I told her our story.

I knew what she meant. 'Why did we put up with her alcoholism?' 'Why did we constantly forgive
her for all of the pain she caused?'

I stood in my place completely stumped. With all the questions, no one had ever asked me 'why' before. I could only muster one answer: "Because we love her." It wasn't a lie, but it didn't fully answer the question.

Just like normal families, we got stuck in a routine but ours was different. My sisters and I would go to school and my parents to work. We'd return home around the same time, get yelled at by my mom because she'd be drunk by two in the afternoon or earlier, argue, escape until the alcohol caused her to pass out, eat dinner, and prepare to do the same routine the next day. What was once an occasional struggle turned into five-or-six-day-a-week siege within a few years.

With age came more involvement in my family's problems. My skin thickened, but my patience wore thin. At any intoxicated mention of my name from my mom, I would fly off the handle. When I got my license, I took full advantage of my sudden ability to run away. Unfortunately, in the process, I selfishly left my sisters to endure the brunt of my mom's attacks.

I took after my dad. When he got mad, he'd jump in his car and drive away without saying a word to avoid worsening the situation. I began doing the same. Typically, that coping mechanism pulled us away from one another until Dad found a way to use it to our advantage. He called it 'escaping the monster.' My mom would relentlessly hurl insults at us until we remembered we had some task we couldn't put off any longer. We did anything to get away from the house: buying paint for one of the rooms, looking for new softball cleats for Angie, or even grocery shopping. Boring errands became our saving grace as we took any opportunity we had to get away. Compared to home, a crowded supermarket was bliss.

Our plan had its faults, though. Neglecting our mom so much caused us to develop more animosity towards her. Between her drunken stupors, she could tell her family was drifting away from her. Still, her addiction had full control and kept her from receiving any help. Our 'escape plan' neglected to address the alcoholism. We were keeping our sanity, but our mom was losing her life.

As we had our routine, she had hers. Up came the sun and down went the vodka. Most of the time, she consumed everything in her path until she passed out. Once top ten of her high school graduating class and a founding member of Philadelphia's Independence Day extravaganza, she was now reduced to a mindless puppet walking barefoot around our town looking for alcohol. She carried around a coin pouch with the only remaining money she had because, while she might be able to keep down a bottle of Tito's vodka, she couldn't hold down a job.

As the years went by and our family's routine became permanent, those one or two days each week that my mom was sober made all the difference. On those days, we were a family again. However, blinded by our bliss, we didn't realize that those were the days our mom got what she needed to fuel her addiction. When Diane would say she was feeling better and promised she would get help, we would stupidly believe her. It happened so infrequently that we latched on to the little bit of hope those words, 'I need help,' brought to us. In turn, we were easily persuaded to give her back her car keys to "look for a job," and lend her money to "just buy cigarettes and some groceries." She wasn't a monster those days, she was our mom. So we were weak and gave in

At the time, Aubrey and I were just young teenagers and didn't yet fully understand the influence our mom was under. On the other hand, my dad did understand, but he couldn't set aside his love for his wife nor ignore the notion that something would click and she'd be back to who she was before the addiction.

Over time, the petty insults blurred into one another and stopped hurting. Unfortunately, every so often my mom did something catastrophic, and the memory was forever seared into our brains. Each time it happened, it was harder for us to answer, "Because we love her."

Vmmmm… Vmmmm. It was my senior year of high school and I was shopping for a last-minute Christmas gift for my girlfriend. My phone vibrated vigorously against the side of my leg, but I ignored the call. Nothing could be more important than the perfect gift for my girlfriend to commemorate our first Christmas together… I was wrong.

Vmmmm… Vmmmm… Vmmmm. After ignoring two calls, my phone continued to vibrate. I angrily ripped it out of my pocket. Who needed to talk to me so bad that they couldn't wait? Dad. I drew a deep breath. It was odd for him to call before his shift ended, but out of all the people I could get away with ignoring, he wasn't one of them.

"H-hello…" I tentatively answered.

"Why the fuck haven't you answered my calls?" he yelled so loud, people around me heard him through the phone. Embarrassed, I walked out of the store ready to be berated.

SCREEEEEACH, I heard the car tires squeal to a stop on the other end of the call, but instead of continuing to yell, my dad's voice changed entirely.

"Ant, I can't talk right now, so listen to me closely. Come to Live and Smile immediately!" CLICK.

I stood outside of the store frozen. Live and Smile was the rehabilitation center in our town. We'd attempted to convince my mom to check in there multiple times, but we had always failed. If my dad was there, it might mean my mom was getting the help she needed. But there was no sense of joy in his voice, only urgency.

Snow started to fall as I jumped in the car and drove towards the least-ventured building in our town. It was off of one of the most crowded roads, but it was rare to see any cars pulling in or out. Nobody wanted to be seen traveling down that rocky entrance-way. When I turned into the campus, I checked to see if I noticed any of my friends' cars on the way. I already felt ashamed when people silently whispered about my mom's addiction behind my back. I would have been mortified if they saw me turning into a rehab center.

Once I entered, snow started falling from the darkening sky. To the right were small houses where the patients stayed. On the left was a large, open lot with construction vehicles, signifying a future expansion. With trees all around, it was tough to see where my dad wanted me to meet him. I read "Admissions" on a newly-formed sign and assumed that following it would lead me in the right direction.

I pulled down a narrow one-lane street. Lost in thought since my dad's call, I forgot I had Christmas music playing in my car until I heard Luther Vandross' "Every Year, Every Christmas." It was our family's favorite Christmas song and always brought about the holiday spirit. This time I only felt angst.

Blinking red and blue lights shone through the trees ahead. As the road gave way to a parking lot, a large, yellow, flat, one-storied building became visible. Multiple cops and ambulances surrounded a crime scene on the far end of the building. Beyond the yellow tape, stood my dad with his hands on his head. Nervous and confused, I crept closer to the commotion. A large object was protruding from the side of the building. Through the snow and the trees, it was tough to identify the object until I walked closer to the scene. It was my mom's car.

"Anthony!" my dad called, waving me towards him. A thousand curious eyes stopped and watched me as I ducked under the police tape. All the while, my eyes were transfixed on our old black SUV. Nearly half of the car had crashed through the cement wall and was inside the building, though I couldn't see what kind of devastation it had caused on the other side. But with all the cars, ambulances, and people, I couldn't imagine that someone hadn't been hit.

"No one was hurt… luckily," my dad said as if he read my mind.

"Thank God," I replied still fixated on the car. "Wh-what happened?"

"Well…" my dad started and stopped as a small smirk briefly appeared on his face. "Your mother finally wanted to get some help."

His words made me smile regardless of the grim situation. My dad managed to handle any predicament we found ourselves in exceptionally well.

A large, bald, middle-aged man approached my dad. He was dressed differently than the other officers, wearing a black polo shirt embroidered with "Township Police" and a holster around his waist. I couldn't put my finger on it, but he looked vaguely familiar.

Without any formal introductions, the man approached my dad and bellowed, "Elliot, it's been too long!"

"Drew, it has. I'm sorry for us meeting again under these circumstances. Thank you for coming," Dad replied.

The man turned to me. "This must be Anthony. Wow, it has been a while since I've seen you.

You're graduating high school this year, right?" he politely asked.

"Yes, sir," I tentatively answered.

"My kids are right behind you in school. Time flies."

"Yes, it does…" My dad jumped in. "Anthony, your mother is waiting alone in a patient room. I told the lady at the front desk you were coming to see her. Only one of us is allowed a brief visit, so please try and calm her down while I talk to Detective Denson."

I nodded. Just as I walked away, the two men ended their trip down memory lane and now had serious looks on their faces. I thought about the name for a few minutes until it dawned on me: Detective Denson coached football against my dad before he rose to prominence in our township's police department.

It wasn't unusual for my dad to know such people. Due to his likable personality and recognizable face, my dad made a ton of important friends: financial advisors, state representatives, a senator, multiple police officers, a lawyer, a doctor, and even the town mayor. He developed relationships with these individuals by volunteering and dedicating time to better the community. In moments like these, such good will was advantageous.

I felt slightly more at ease knowing Detective Denson had come to help. Nevertheless, the severity of the situation hit me as I was led down an isolated part of the building by an older lady who worked the front desk. Most of the workers had been cleared from the building and all of the patients directed back to their rooms, so the hallway was empty except for one light.

A nurse stepped out of the room to tell me my mom was shaken up but had not sustained any major injuries.

She allowed me into the room but told me I only had five minutes to talk to my mom. Nervously, I entered the room not knowing whether I'd be greeted by the monster yelling "Fuck you" or my mom saying "I'm sorry." To my surprise, it was the latter.

Mom lay on a hospital bed with her back to me, staring at the wall. As I approached, I saw tears streaming down her face.

"Why, Mom?" I asked as I sat down in a chair beside her.

She had no answer. She just shook her head and continued to look in the opposite direction. I placed my hand on hers and she shuddered. "Why do you keep doing this to us? Why do you keep doing this to yourself?" I tried again sympathetically.

"I don't know, Anthony. I... can't... stop..." she sobbed.

I exhaled to expel some of my anger. As pissed off as I was, I had to try and remain calm. 'I can't stop' was the closest she had ever been to admitting she struggled with addiction. If I used my time wisely, maybe she'd be willing to receive help.

"What happened?" I inquired so she could corroborate what I assumed.

My mom let out a deep breath between tears. Finally, she explained: "I was feeling depressed and wanted to get out of the house. Your aunt and I haven't been talking and I needed help, so I made a right into Live and Smile instead of a left into her neighborhood. Next thing I knew, I was in this bed and your father was telling me I crashed."

"Mom, it wasn't an accidental car crash... You drove straight through the building." I couldn't help correcting her. "Did you drink?"

My mom didn't answer. She turned away again and cried harder, so I asked again, "Did you drink?"

"I just had one drink," she lied.

"I'll ask you one more time: Did you drink?"

"I told you before, I only had one drink. I was depressed and stopped by the bar for a few minutes. Ask the bartender how many I had."

"You drove your car through a rehabilitation center! How can you dare lie to my face about how many drinks you had?!" I yelled, standing over the bed, my face red with rage.

"I drank a lot, okay? I was drunk and crashed. It's my fault! Is that what you wanted to hear?!" my mom wailed.

After finally hearing the truth, my anger subsided. I didn't know much about addiction, but I knew that admitting she had a problem was the key to her finding treatment. I settled back in my chair ready to be more productive in preparing my mom to accept help, but I was too late.

"Time's up; you have to leave now," said a nurse in the doorway.

"No, not yet. Please let my son stay with me," my mom pleaded.

The nurse shook her head sternly. My mom grabbed my arm and looked me in the eyes. "Anthony, don't let them take me away. I need to be home for Christmas..."

"I'm sorry but you need to leave," the nurse repeated. "We'll take care of your mom."

I looked down at my mother. Despite running her car into the side of a building while black-out drunk, she was physically unscathed. Now she lay in the bed confused and crying with the hope I could save her. But I couldn't, not this time. I didn't have the energy nor the knowledge to help her in such a serious situation. Regardless of my anger and my disappointment, I hugged her tightly and confidently promised, "We will make sure you are home for Christmas."

A small smile curled on her face as I was leaving. I couldn't imagine our favorite holiday without her.

When I reached the parking lot again, my dad was talking to a couple of people not associated with the police department. He immediately sent me back home until he could get the situation 'under control.'

Aubrey and Angie couldn't believe the story. When I got home, they asked me a ton of questions I couldn't answer. I just told them that Dad had a plan. He did. A couple of hours later, he arrived and sat us all down in the living room like he typically did when he wanted to discuss an important family issue.

He explained how he was friends with Detective Denson and how he was able to get all of the charges against our mom dropped. However, he had been unsuccessful convincing the rehabilitation center to release our mom from their care. With only days until our family's Christmas Eve gathering, my dad would 'have to' heroically rescue mom so she was with her family.

After all of the harm her alcoholism had caused in the past and particularly that day, it felt wrong to pull my mom from necessary help, but when I gave my dad my support in his decision, only one piece of advice stuck in my head: addicts have to want help in order to receive help. My mom didn't willingly go for help, so it felt like the right decision having her home for Christmas. The next day, miraculously, there she was. My dad had succeeded. Tears of joy filled my mom's eyes as she sobbed, "I will never drink again."

The five of us celebrated all day with Christmas music, movies, cookies, and card games. It was the best time we had spent together in a while. On Christmas Eve, we started our usual tradition: my mom made a dish to bring to her sister's house, my sisters wrapped the gifts, and my dad and I drove to pick Grandma Palma up from her house.

Usually, the trip to Grandma's was spent deep in conversation about the effects of Mom's alcoholism, and we'd develop an escape plan for my grandma if my mom was drunk. This ride, we sang along to Christmas music and talked about my upcoming baseball season.

As usual, when we picked her up, my grandma asked a few questions about my mom's alcoholism. It was clear she was expecting bad news. But this time when she asked, I just replied with a smile, "Good."

She gave an incredulous glance in my direction. We rarely had good news about my mom's state. But my dad and I had decided we would only deliver the positive strides my mom was making and neglect to mention what had caused the epiphany.

"Grandma, we won't have any problems this time around. We actually think something clicked and my mom won't drink," I promised. I wasn't lying. At that moment, I really felt my mom was sincere. She had seen the severity of her addiction and had made the choice to be stronger for her family.

Nevertheless, my grandma was skeptical. "I hope so..." she said, her voice trailing off. "It's just hard to believe that. Each time I want to, your mom drinks again."

"I know, Ma." my dad said. "We feel the same way, but Diane asked me today to take her to join an outpatient rehabilitation program after the holidays."

My grandma grinned briefly. "Let's just have a great Christmas together."

We played our favorite Christmas song on the radio and sang along. We finally felt positive during a holiday.

Then my phone rang, and Aubrey's name popped up on the screen while my phone was still connected to the car speakers for everyone to hear.

"Hel—" I started before Aubrey cut in.

"Ant, w-where are you? It's m-mom again," she said, her voice shaking.

I yanked my phone off of the auxiliary cord in hopes of minimizing what my grandma could hear. Dad turned to me with a grave look on his face. Aubrey talked in one ear as my dad asked "What happened?" in the other.

Finally, Aubrey hit me with it. "Mom's d-drunk," she stuttered as if saying the words made it all too real.

My mouth dropped open. I was at a loss for words. Aubrey kept calling my name, but I couldn't talk. My dad shook his head. He had read my body language and assumed right. Still, we left my grandma in the dark, hoping to salvage the slightest bit of optimism.

Being Christmas Eve, we couldn't 'escape the monster' like we usually did. Instead, we went into 'Control Mode.' That meant we had to do whatever necessary to keep my mom from drinking anymore. Quietly, I gave Aubrey the instructions over the phone: scour the house for hidden bottles of vodka, keep mom from leaving, convince her to take a nap, and refrain from arguing with her whatsoever. "If she discovers you're trying to sober her up, she'll definitely find a way to drink, so don't be obvious."

Aubrey listened and agreed to do what she could. I hung up hoping she had made a mistake in identifying mom's state.

She hadn't.

When we got home, my mom stumbled through the open front door slurring, "Hey Ma!" as she gave my grandma a hug. Grandma tentatively accepted but looked at my dad and I dumbfounded. There was no doubt in my mind now. After running her car through the side of a rehab center drunk, narrowly avoiding arrest, being admitted into a rehab facility two days before Christmas, and returning home promising never to drink again, Mom was drunk. The power of her addiction never ceased to amaze me.

In a matter of seconds, I broke the golden rule of 'Control Mode' and poked the beehive. "I can't believe you're drunk. What is wrong with you?" I hissed at my mom as I walked by her into the house.

Luckily, I only heard a few insults mumbled under her breath. If she was riled up too much, another holiday could have been ruined. Fortunately, with a little bit of luck, we narrowly avoided any major issues before leaving the house.

In the car ride to my aunt's house, though, Diane tried to push us to our limit and bait us into an argument. "Don't look at me like that, Elliot. Remember your temper is the reason we had a falling-out with my brother-in-law and sister," she said spitefully, loud enough for the whole car to hear.

My grandma grimaced but bit her tongue. My sisters and I did not have her patience. Aubrey made a snide comment, and Diane turned her anger towards her daughter, claiming our cousins hated her.

Whether it was friends, family, or each other, Diane always attempted to pit people against one another. By doing so, she felt that people would neglect to be mad at her for being drunk and direct their anger elsewhere.

Finally, we made it to the Christmas Eve gathering without any major arguments. Our mom was still drunk, but less noticeably.

We were still in 'Control Mode,' so my sisters and I remained near our mom, being overly nice to her. By watching over her shoulder, we could minimize the insults and lies she would tell about us to our family.

Normally, we cherished the one night we could see our aunts, uncles, and cousins. Unfortunately, that night we had to spend more time trying to control the situation than hanging out with our family.

Finally, we decided to leave.

"I can't believe we made it through that," Aubrey whispered to me, relieved, as we walked outside.

On the car ride home, we noticed our mom was finally sober and well into the Christmas spirit. We decided to leave her be. We were too exhausted to call her out on her drinking and respected our grandma too much to do that in front of her.

As I lay in bed that night, one word lingered in my mind: family. Everyone in our family knew of our mom's addiction, but nobody spoke of it. Some of our family members chose to even distance themselves from the issue, and as a result, they distanced themselves from us. My sisters and I felt totally isolated. We loved our family, and it crushed us not to be close like we once were.

But that's when I realized, family is not dictated by blood. It is determined by the people who are there for you, not only through the best of times but the worst of times as well.

I thought of my parents' best friends who gave me a place to sleep and a willing ear when I needed it. I thought of my Poppie, his wife (who became a second grandma), and the part of the family that braved my mom's alcoholism to attend every one of our gatherings no matter what. I thought of my best friends who took the time out of their holidays, like always, to text me words of encouragement and bits of advice. I thought of my girlfriend, Taylor, who would be over the next day bearing a ton of gifts and an infectious smile, knowing full well she could be greeted by my mom intoxicated. I thought about her family and how they welcomed me immediately with open arms. I thought about Aubrey, Angie, my dad, my grandma, and even my mom when she was sober. The memories we shared were irreplaceable, and in truth, I was never alone. I always had family.

With those thoughts, I drifted off to sleep, and I woke up Christmas morning with my mom running around the house bright-eyed and bushy-tailed. She was making breakfast, playing music, and setting up presents around the tree. All that day, it seemed the thought of drinking never crossed her mind. We had a fantastic Christmas and never mentioned the chaos that had transpired days prior.

The next day, we started our routine all over again.

SEVEN

Sympathy for the Devil

Her car is nowhere to be seen. I find her standing on the edge of a wooded area behind the elementary school with three cops around her, leaves and sticks in her hair from hiding in the nearby shrubbery. Her shirt is now a combination of dirt and dried blood. The child-sized green shorts have a rip on the side revealing more of her torn-up legs. Her eyes grow to twice their size as I approach.

"Hi, mom…" I say, tentatively walking in her direction.

Her voice quivers as she asks Officer Barley, "W-what's he d-d-doing here?"

Confused, he answers, "That's your son. I called him to meet us here so he can take you home."

"No, no, I can't go home with him. I can't!" Diane responds as she hides behind one of the other officers. "H-he beats m-me."

My mouth drops open in disbelief. I've never hit my mom in my life, but I shouldn't be surprised. Diane will do anything to take the blame off herself, even if it means lying to get me in trouble with the law.

"Does he now?" Officer Barley asks, glaring in my direction.

"Yes, yes he does," Diane says with a grin showing her yellow and rotting teeth. "He has a mean streak just like his father. This innocent thing is just an act. He broke our door frame, our screen door, and even gave his sister a black eye. It's no wonder his girlfriend wants to leave him."

Diane's smile is bigger than her face as I stand frozen in place. My hands are shaking, my blood is boiling, and my fists are clenched. The monster accomplished exactly what she intended: all three officers are looking directly at me.

I want to argue my innocence, but I can't. Other than my girlfriend wanting to leave me, every other word she said is true. I do have a mean streak. I have broken things in the house—more than I can count—and my anger unintentionally hurt Aubrey in the past. But the only time my anger gets the best of me is when my mom is drunk and carrying on. Her barrage of insults day in and day out pushes me to my wit's end.

Diane looks around gleaming; the attention is off of her now. "Arrest him!" she exclaims. "I'm not the one with a problem, he is with his temper. He needs to be sent away for anger management."

I let out a sigh. She has the upper hand and if I fight back, I'll just be proving her right. I continue to stand silent hoping Officer Barley sees through her lies.

"Okay, we'll take your word for it. Get in my car and we'll take you home. I'm sure one of your daughters will back up your story. Then, we can have a different conversation with your son," the officer says to my surprise.

She agrees as another cop leads her to the back of his car. Then, Officer Barley turns his attention to me. "We'll get this all straightened out; we just need to get your mom home. Why don't you meet us there?"

I nod and start to walk back towards my house. My heart is pounding and my arms are sweaty as I jog through a short-cut in hopes of reaching my sisters before the cops do. I assume they will have my back, but I'm still worried the police will catch Aubrey by surprise or that she will still be upset about the black eye.

One day, my mom turned her usual drunken anger on me. I couldn't take the abuse, so I reacted by launching a full bottle of water in the air over my mom's head careful not to hit anyone. I hoped to scare her enough for her to stop insulting me, but I threw it just as fast as any pitch I've ever thrown in baseball. The bottle bounced off of a cabinet, flew over my shoulder, and hit Aubrey square in the eye. It all happened so quickly, but before I knew it, Aubrey was laying on the ground whimpering from the pain. Everyone yelled at me and I felt horrible, but soon after, we all laughed it off. I hope Aubrey is still laughing…

When I reach the house, the three cop cars sit outside, their lights inconspicuously flickering into all of our neighbors' windows. Some doors are open as neighbors have come out to see the commotion. In the middle of the street, my dad stares gaping at my mom being escorted out of the back of one of the cars.

"What happened?" he asks as I approach him.

"We had to call the cops," I answer. "Mom attempted—"

My dad cuts me off before I can explain. "Look at this scene. All of our neighbors are sure getting a good view. We're a fucking circus act and everyone is coming to see. Now the whole town will know," he grunts.

I say nothing. I simply turn red because he's right. I didn't know what to do, so I involved the police. I start to explain, "I just thought maybe this could help M—"

"Do you know how embarrassing this is? How could you think this would help?" he asks. "I'm 55 years old and I have to deal with this?! Well, guess what? I'm fucking DONE!"

With anger bursting through his veins, my dad storms towards my mom. "What the fuck are you doing, Diane?" he yells as my mother heads up the walkway to the house.

"Good, you're here," my mom snaps back, turning to walk back toward him. "The cops are here for you, Elliot. They're finally going to arrest you!" The two stride towards one another like two prizefighters at a press conference.

"Arrest me?!" my dad yells. "Look at yourself. You're a drunken mess. Look at what you're doing to yourself. Look at what you're doing to your family!

"I'm not the one who goes out every weekend and drinks. I don't do anything wrong!"

"Don't do anything wrong? You're lucky I don't..." My dad stops mid-sentence after realizing he is face-to-face with two officers instead of his wife. The size difference between my parents suddenly becomes noticeable. I see why the officers are nervous. Little do they know that my mom's weapon is all mental and no muscles stand a chance against her constant belittling.

"Is there any way you could take her away?" my dad asks the cops.

"We'll talk about the situation privately, sir," Officer Barley answers. "Diane promised to go inside and lay down. Right?"

My mom starts to shake when everyone turns their attention to her. She quietly answers 'no' and hides behind the other officer. "I can't go inside if he is going to be there," she says, pointing a finger at my dad.

"Why?" Officer Barley asks. The crowd of onlookers grows quiet to hear the answer.

"HE BEATS ME! MY HUSBAND BEATS ME! ARREST HIM... HE BEATS ME!" Diane wails.

My dad stands frozen in place, fuming. "I didn't fucking touch you!" he bursts out.

Diane's fear washes away as she notices the attention turned to my dad. "That's not what I told your boss today when I called him," she retaliates with a smirk.

"My boss? You better not...I'm the only person who makes any money for this family! You're going to jeopardize our livelihood with a lie?" he asks her.

"Well, I made more money than YOU! You couldn't even hold down a job and I supported you!"

"Diane, that was 20 years ago! Now look at you; you're a mess. You couldn't hold down a janitor job. Look at all the people here watching you. Can't you see what you're doing to our family?" I can hear the pain in my dad's voice as he hopes to somehow get through to her.

Instead, Diane moves nearly nose-to-nose with him and snarls, "They're here to see you, Elliot. They know how much of a fat slob and loser you are. They all hate you just like I hate you..."

My dad's nostrils flare like a bull's. He's so mad, he can't speak.

Ha Ha Ha! Diane lets out a blood-curdling laugh then says, "You're disgusting."

Just as my dad opens his mouth to retaliate, my mom spits in his face.

Before my dad can react, Officer Barley quickly steps between them and pulls my mom away. I grab my dad, but he shrugs me off. Officer Barley whispers something to my mom as another cop approaches. Finally, my mom turns and starts for our front door.

"Why does she get to go back into my house?" my dad asks the officer.

"I understand your frustration, but she agreed to go straight to bed. I think that would be best for everyone right now," he answers.

"Why is that best for ME or for MY family? Why should she be allowed to walk back into my house after all she just did?" my dad tries again.

"Sir, she did not break any law, so there's nothing more we can do," he replies.

My dad's face turns from anger to disappointment.

"Let's gather up your kids and talk about the options your family does have," Officer Barley suggests. My dad agrees and we walk inside.

"Where's mom?" I whisper to Aubrey when we get inside.

"She's in bed. Ang and I watched the whole scene from the window, but we couldn't hear everything. What's happening?" she asks.

"I have no idea. I think we're about to find out, but mom isn't getting arrested."

Aubrey's face falls. She immediately turns to Angie and says something in her ear. Ang lets out a sigh.

My dad, my sisters, and I all sit down in our living room. Typically, Dad holds our family meetings. It's weird to see someone else presiding over one this time.

"So let me begin the only way I can," Officer Barley starts. "I'm not sure if you're aware, but in the state of Pennsylvania, no person can be forced into rehabilitation."

"We're aware," Ang responds.

"Good. Your mother did not do anything illegal, so we can't arrest her or bring her into a rehab facility."

With that statement, he lost any shred of patience we had.

"She was drinking and driving. We even gave you her license plate number. Why can't you arrest her for that?" Aubrey argues.

"We didn't catch your mother driving any vehicle while intoxicated. We didn't see her car in the area when we found her," Officer Barley responds.

We all shake our heads in disbelief. "Teflon Diane…" my dad says under his breath.

The officer gives him a puzzled look.

"That's what we call my wife," my dad explains. "No matter how much damage she causes, she gets out of it."

The officer half-heartedly nods his head. It's tough for an outsider to fully comprehend our situation. To us, our mom seems nearly invincible. For the last five years, she's driven drunk almost every day. Despite the 1.5 million drunk-driving arrests per year, she's never been caught—even when we give the cops her license plate number and location.

Officer Barley clears his throat. "I'll be honest with you all, your options are slim. Your first and most likely option is to convince her she has a problem. If you could do that, she could sign herself into a rehabilitation center."

We all take a deep breath.

"I'm sorry," I respond, "but I don't think that's an option right now. I've driven my mom to rehab centers and had her talk on the phone with people that can help. All it did was add fuel to the fire."

"Right," my dad chimes in. "I've even tried filming her drunk and playing it back to her when she was sober since she blacks out. I hoped it would help her realize the damage she causes and how often. Instead, she refuses to watch the videos or doesn't believe they are real. In the end, it usually causes her to drink more."

"I understand. And that's why there are two other options, but I caution you, they are difficult to achieve and could result in forcing your mom into a 'help' program. I know that sounds ideal for you all, but forcing help on an addict who does not believe she has a problem could turn out to be completely counterproductive and disastrous," Office Barley warns us.

We all let his advice sink in, but after the day we've had, help is help regardless of what my mom wants or the form it comes in.

Ang quickly breaks the silence, "What are the options?"

Officer Barley nods and presses on, "The second option is a 302B. Most of the time, it is a plea that has to be filled out at a hospital and approved by a judge. Alone, addiction does not merit approval to force somebody in to help. You have to be able to prove mental illness and that Diane is a danger to herself or others."

"That's most of the time," I cut in. "What is the other way a person could fall under that category?"

"The other way is slightly rarer in your situation, but possible. If your mom threatened or acted on a threat to harm herself or others in front of a police officer, she would immediately be escorted to a hospital for evaluation. After that, she'll more than likely be placed in a mental health facility," Officer Barley answers.

"Even drunk, Diane's too smart for that," my dad replies. "Is there a third option?"

The officer starts to explain the long and tedious process of being approved by the state for a restraining order and its implications. I zone out and grow fixated on the second option. My mom threatened to commit suicide all day, but never in front of an officer. She is a master at avoiding trouble. In addition, she lied about her cut, so I couldn't use the evidence to prove she was a danger to herself. The police considered Aubrey's hand an accident and it was not enough to prove my mom attempted suicide. Nevertheless, my mom is sobering up with each minute we waste talking. She never acted as reckless as she has today. Now is the time for help, not tomorrow, and not after our vacation... now.

I sneak away from the group and walk upstairs. I try to open the door to my parents' bedroom, but it's locked. Lightly, so no one downstairs will hear, I knock and call for my mom. No answer. I try again a little louder.

"What, what do you want? I'm sleeping!" Diane slurs through the cracks in the door.

"Mom, come downstairs. We want to talk to you," I answer back.

The door swings open. Diane stands in front of me with her bloody shirt, hair a mess, ripped pants, and still noticeably drunk.

"Is your father down there?" she asks. "And what about that cop?"

"No, the officer left, but Dad is downstairs and wants to talk to you," I bait her.

"Good, because I have a lot to say to him," she says as she starts to stagger down the stairs behind me. Too easy.

"I... uh... have to go to the bathroom," my mom lies.

"Wait!" I call out, but it is too late. Before I can turn to stop her, she has already turned and ascended the stairs and headed into the bathroom. Since underneath the bathroom sink is her favorite hiding spot for a liter bottle of vodka, there is no doubt she ran back in for some liquid courage before confronting my dad.

I keep one ear towards the stairs listening for Office Barley and another listening for the familiar sound of my mom taking swigs out of the bottle. After a minute, I give up waiting.

Knock, Knock, Knock! "Dad's looking for you, are you okay mom?" I politely ask so I don't stir the pot too much. We both know why she locked herself in the bathroom.

"I'll uh, be out in a minute," she responds. I hear the toilet flush—her lame attempt at masking her drinking. Still, one swig follows another.

I pace back and forth on the landing at the top of our stairs, growing more impatient with each passing minute. "I know why you're really in there! Stop drinking!" I yell into the door. BANG! The plastic bottle slams against the wall as the door finally swings open.

"I was going to the goddamn bathroom," Diane slurs, "What the hell do you want with me?"

"I told you before you went in there to drink. Dad needs to talk to you downstairs, right now!" I answer. She snarls in my direction but heads downstairs.

I hurry past my mom to survey the situation. It is too quiet.

"Where's Officer Barley?" I ask in a panic.

"He and the other officers left," my dad answers. "Why?"

A sense of defeat runs through me. I awakened the beast again, and for nothing.

Before I can explain my misguided plan, a voice from behind me yells, "FUCK YOU, Elliot!"

EIGHT

Lean on Me

CRASH! Pieces of shattered glass from our storm door rained over my body like snow on a winter's day. My fist bled profusely as I stood hunched over on the front step of my house shaking and crying. Taylor, who was walking in front of me, turned around and immediately held me in a long embrace.

"It'll be okay," she whispered as she wiped shards of glass out of my hair.

"That's what you get," Diane snarled from inside the doorway.

"What the fuck is wrong with you!" my dad yelled at my mom as he pushed her aside to check on me.

My sisters, who were crying from the fight, screamed at our mom from inside the house too. With tears rolling down her face, Angie wailed, "Look at what you're doing to us. Get out of our house! Get out of our lives! Can't you see we don't want you here?!"

"Fine, I will," Diane responded while walking out of the doorway and through the broken glass barefoot. As she passed me sitting on the front step, she whispered for only Taylor and I to hear, "I fucking hate you, Anthony." Moments later, she disappeared disheveled and bleeding into a stretch of trees near our house.

Taylor stepped away to check on my sisters, so my dad sat down next to me. With his arm around my shoulder, he joked, "You really have a knack for breaking things in our house, huh?"

I briefly cracked a smile.

"Anthony, you are my first born child and I will always love you. I didn't have a good relationship with my father, so I'm very lucky that we're close. I don't want any of this to come between us."

I nodded. I appreciated what he said, but I was not in the mood to talk.

"This is not fair what you and your sisters are going through," he continued, "but I want you to know that I'll always be here for you. I promise I will make this right, so we will never have to go through something like this again."

I shook my head, stood up, and finally answered him. "Dad, I have to go. I can't be around this house right now. I'll see you soon... I guess." I knew my response hurt him because he hated seeing me leave, especially after something like that. But I needed to be away from there, to be back at my apartment at college, not knowing when I'd build the courage to return home again.

"I understand," he somberly responded, then pulled me in for a hug. "I love you, son."

Taylor overheard our conversation and already had our bags out front. My sisters both awkwardly hugged me, then I turned around and Taylor and I got into my car. With tears rolling down my cheeks, I drove away unable to bear looking at my family, but I knew they were crying, too.

Our one-hour car ride felt never-ending. The crying subsided but I remained silent. Taylor didn't push me to let out my feelings. Instead, she occasionally squeezed my hand to let me know she was there. It was exactly what I needed at the time.

A half hour into our trip, I felt compelled to pour my emotions out. "My own mother wished me dead today," I stated solemnly. "She looked me in the eyes and told me I'll never amount to anything."

Taylor simply reached over to put her hand on my shoulder and listened intently.

"She called me ugly, a loser, and a mistake. Then, she had the audacity to turn her anger at you. babe, I'm so sorry..." I started to cry again.

"Anthony, you have nothing to be sorry about. I love your mom, and I love you," Taylor responded with a comforting smile on her face.

"But it's not fair. It's just not fair!" I yelled back.

"I know it's not. It's not fair to you at all," she said, squeezing my hand again.

I let out a deep sigh and tried to compose myself. "It's not me that I'm worried about. I despise being insulted by my mom, but I have to be stronger than that. I didn't run my fist through a glass door because of what she said. I've heard it all before.

"I've never been there for anything like this before, so I totally understand how you reacted, but what caused it?" Taylor asked.

"I didn't yell back at her this time," I answered slowly. "Instead, I tried to get her to recognize what she was doing, so I asked her how much she loves me. As a kid, she used to ask me, 'How much does Mommy love you?'

I'd smile and eagerly spread my arms out to show her. Then she would grab me and hug me. Even as I got older, when she did that, I felt how strong of a bond we shared. But when I asked this time, I was met with, 'Fuck you, I never loved you.' That hurt worse than any insult she could have thrown because it shows how quickly I'm losing my mother."

My face was flushed, and when I looked at Taylor, tears were rolling down her face. She quietly said, "I know it may not seem like it, but your mom loves you."

"I know…" I said, keeping my eyes on the road, lost in thought. "I just can't let her lose this fight. Even now, I can't stop wondering if she's okay. She ran away barefoot and bleeding. I just want to turn my car around and go find her but I can't. It's so hard to keep my distance while being her strength. Between the insults and the failed attempts at breaking through to her, I'm emotionally drained. Regardless, I can't stop fighting. Even if it means breaking one hundred more glass doors and enduring a thousand more insults, I can't lose my mom to addiction."

Taylor reached for my right hand and kissed it. She held onto it and whispered lovingly, "Then you won't be fighting alone. I will always be here for your family and I will always be here for you."

I was grateful for Taylor and everyone in our corner. Even when I felt completely hopeless, I was surrounded by love. If I could help my mom realize that, too, maybe I could save her life.

NINE

You're Not My God

"Fuck me? What have I ever done to you, Diane?!" Elliot yells, not missing a beat.

"You lie, you cheat, and you beat me. You're doing to me exactly what you did to your first wife!"

"That was thirty-five years ago! How could you continue to badger me for having an ex-wife that long ago?"

Diane stumbles into a wall as she slowly approaches my dad. "Ha! You're so ugly, Elliot. No one ever really loved you or ever will again," she slurs in his face as spit flies all over.

My dad attempts to respond with civility so the night doesn't get any worse, "Diane, please stop this. Our kids need their mother and you're hurting them by constantly acting this way."

"You didn't even think they were human until they were three. How could you say I'm ruining this family when you didn't even want kids?" We've heard this one before. Diane often recycles insults she knows hurts us.

My dad takes a step back from his wife and draws a deep breath. No matter how close she just was to being arrested, she hasn't learned a thing. He can tell. She's getting worse. There won't be any civility, and we're running out of options.

Typically, my mom ends her tirades by sneaking off to drink from a hidden bottle until she passes out. Tonight, it seems as though she won't stop until she crushes everyone's soul.

As my dad stares past her in thought, she renews her attacks, "What the fuck are you staring at?" My dad doesn't humor her with a response. "You are too stupid to answer. Well, fuck you, Elliot. You're ugly, stupid, and a waste. The wrong brother died. THE WRONG FUCKING BROTHER!"

My dad closes his eyes and clenches his fists. Diane struck the ultimate nerve. This is what she used earlier in the day to upset him enough to leave. Aubrey and Ang didn't realize how much it had hurt him, but I did. His brother passed away around the same time as my mom-mom. He was young, only forty-five. They were extremely close, even though my uncle lived on the other side of the country, but after an illustrious career with the Air Force and NASA, my uncle accepted a job in New York City and was moving back home. My dad couldn't have been more excited. During the medical screening for the position, doctors found a tumor on my uncle's brain. After a few years of fighting, cancer won, beating the toughest man my dad ever knew.

My mom responded to the loss of her mother by drinking. My dad took comfort in spending more time with his family. After her own experience with grief, she must understand how difficult it still is for him, but drunk, it's her ultimate weapon against him.

Aubrey comes to bat for my dad. "Screw you, Mom. Don't talk to Dad like that. He's actually a parent, unlike YOU!" she yells.

"And you're so innocent? I see the way you dress and the pictures you take," Diane snickers.

"What are you talking about?" Aubrey responds.

"No one is ever going to love you, no matter how much you try. You're a slut," she snaps. She has a short memory because the last time she used that insult today, she landed on her ass.

This time, Angie steps in for Aubrey. "Stop it, Mom. Don't say that about her! You know it's not true!"

"Fuck you, too!" Diane shouts at her youngest daughter. "You aren't wanted; you aren't wanted by anyone. That's why your boyfriend left you!"

That's it. I decide I can't take it anymore. Angie has just experienced her first heartbreak, and she doesn't have to be reminded of it. I decide to step in and take the brunt of the attack. Diane will try to hit me with her best insult, and I'll be ready to give it right back.

"Don't you dare talk to my sisters that way!" I scream.

"Ha Ha Ha! And what the fuck are you going to do?" Diane taunts. "You're just as ugly as your father. Taylor is going to leave you as soon as she realizes how much of a fucking loser you are," she barks back.

Her insult doesn't work. I'm ready with something tougher. "You have a drinking problem because your mom is dead! You don't realize that your own family doesn't want you anymore? They HATE you. That's why you never see or hear from them anymore. You FAILED your own mother!"

Rather than crying like I expected, Diane punches me in the chest. Caught off guard, I take a step back, but she moves forward. With tears in her eyes, she looks to unleash all of her anger on me. But as I'm backed into a corner with my mom continually smacking me, I smile at her. It's a grin of disbelief and sudden realization.

My mom looks at me and snickers, "What the fuck do you think is so funny?" I notice the whole room is pondering the same question.

"Mom, you can't physically hurt me. You can't physically hurt any of us. Whatever pain you're trying to inflict, you've already done so tenfold without laying a finger on us. We have scars that will last a lifetime. I know you're drunk because our mother is too smart and too kind to think hitting her children will accomplish anything."

My explanation falls flat and is met with a sinister grin of no understanding and a few more blows to my chest.

"Hit me all you want!" I continue in a rage. "It's not going to solve one goddamn problem!" I yell. "It won't change the fact that you were raped or that you were sent to live with your grandparents! It's not going to change the fact that your mom is DEAD! She moved on and while you wallow in self-pity, we're losing our mom, too! YOU NEED TO MOVE ON!"

Tears roll down her face, and I realize I have finally broken through. But then, I take it one step too far: "You're an alcoholic and you're tearing your family apart. You need help!"

Before I can realize it, the monster takes full control of my mom again. SMACK! Her hand connects with the side of my face. My dad runs over and grabs her by the arms in an attempt to pull her away.

"Don't you fucking touch my son!" he demands. Before he has the opportunity to carry her away, my mom spits in my face and screams back, "He's no son of mine!"

Anger pulses through all of us. My dad drops my mom on the living room floor. "What the fuck is wrong with you?!" he bellows.

"Fuck you, Elliot! FUCK YOU! FUCK YOU! FUCK YOU!" Diane screams back with that same sinister grin spread across her face. It's a look that says, 'I could hurt you much worse than you can hurt me.'

My dad looks like he is out for blood as the last ten years boil up beyond his breaking point. As he starts towards my mom, I quickly step in and push him back.

"Get the fuck out of my way, Anthony!" he commands while pushing my arms away.

"Don't let her make you do something stupid. She wants you to do that!" I reply, trying to reason with him as Diane stands behind me laughing.

"I don't give a fuck what she's trying to do. She's killing our family!" my dad answers. "Why are you protecting her?!"

Rather than waiting to hear my answer to his question, he continues to try to push through me. In response, I scream to get his attention, "STOP BEING A FUCKING SELF-CENTERED IDIOT AND LISTEN TO ME!"

Blind-sided by the insult, my dad winds his fist up and threatens me. "I should knock your fucking teeth out for talking to me like that!"

"Go ahead. Do it. But nobody is dealing with Mom that way. We're doing it the right way," I calmly reply.

My dad grabs me by the collar of my shirt with his fist still wound up, then suddenly lets go. He exhales loudly and his anger subsides.

I use this opportunity to answer his question: "You want to know why I protect Mom? Well, she may be your wife and, yes, you may still love her, but she is OUR MOM. She gave birth to us and raised us. When we were sick, she took care of us. When we needed a hand to hold, there she was. When we were scared, she gave us courage. That monster that has taken over her body is not our mom. Our mom is the most beautiful, caring, and understanding woman in the world. And that person is still in there somewhere, so I will fight every single day to get her back. All three of us will. You're either with us or against us."

My dad looks down at the floor disappointed in himself. "Anthony, I'm sorry. You know I'm always with you guys. You three are my entire life. But I'm at my wit's end and I don't know what I'm going to do anymore…"

I answer promptly and loud enough for my mom to hear my plan clearly, "I know what we are going to do; we will call the cops back. They have their limits, too. Let's use that as an opportunity to get OUR mom, not this monster, the help she needs, whether she likes it or not."

At the mention of 'cops,' my mom, who had been sitting idly while the attention was not on her, bursts out, "No, don't you dare call the cops. I swear to god, I'll really kill myself this time. I'll really do it. Don't you dare call the cops, Anthony!" she threatens.

More calmly than he's been all night, my dad replies, "I'm sorry, Diane, but we have to. I'll be the one to call this time." He takes out his phone and dials 911.

"I'm getting the fuck out of here!" the monster yells as she springs to her feet and through the front door catching us all off guard.

"Let her go," my dad directs my sisters and I.

"Not tonight, Dad. Call the cops and I'll catch her. This night will be different." I assure him.

I open the front door to a dark and quiet nothingness. For the first time all night, our street is peaceful and not littered with cop lights and gossiping neighbors. With such a shitty day, how can the night sky be so beautiful? I want to enjoy it, but I know that isn't possible. Not yet.

I comb the street looking for a disheveled drunk lady attempting to hide. Near some trees in the corner of the street, I see my mom ducking behind a car. I start in her direction, but she notices me and darts towards the busiest intersection in our town.

I sprint after her, closing in on her easily.

"I'm going to run in front of a fucking car!" she threatens. "I WANT TO DIE!"

I may be fast, but I am still 80 feet from her as she nears the intersection, our footsteps whispering through the grass before the street. I can hear the cars rushing by ahead and my heartbeat begins bursting through my chest. My mom approaches the intersection with headlights highlighting her frail frame. In the distance, a tractor-trailer blows its horn. My mom takes a step into the street and closes her eyes. HONK! HONK! HONK! The tractor-trailer driver blows his horn as my mom's whole silhouette is highlighted by the lights.

Before she can achieve her own end, I grab her and hold her in a bear hug. I lift her up and carry her away from the road and toward our house.

"Anthony, p-please l-l-let me die," my mom sobs as she kicks at my shins to get loose.

"It's not your time, Mom," I calmly reply as we struggle towards home. For once, the blue and red lights of the cop cars are a welcoming sight. I'm optimistic they can help after the night we've had and all they've endured with us. Three times in one day has to be a new record for a family.

Officer Cici, the short blonde cop, steps out of the car as I'm shoving my mom in her direction. She quickly acknowledges us and signals another officer to follow her. My mom panics but I have too tight of a grip on her arms for her to move anywhere but forward.

"As soon as I heard the call came from your house, I came right away," Officer Cici says. "Please let me talk to your mom briefly, and then I'll be in to talk to your family."

I take a deep breath in frustration but nod my head in agreement. After half of the police force swarmed my neighborhood and after so many calls, I cannot believe the civility she has towards my mom. I feel like screaming at her, but that won't do anyone any good, so I bite my tongue and walk inside to join my family.

They are already standing out front, and I update them on what just happened and what the officer said. Rather than arguing or getting upset, we decide to sit in the living room and wait.

For ten minutes, nobody says a word until the screen door swings open, and Mom walks in followed by Officer Cici and another cop. Tears flow out of her eyes as she woefully walks by us without making eye contact. As she is walking up the stairs towards her bedroom, the officers start to explain the situation.

"I spoke with Diane. She agreed to go straight to bed. I told her I have no problem putting her in cuffs if she doesn't call it a night. The only issue is, that was an empty threat. I can't arrest her because she hasn't done anything wrong…"

Aubrey breaks in and impatiently asks what we all are thinking, "Can you do anything for us?"

Officer Cici sighs and apologizes. "No, I'm sorry. Legally, there's nothing we can do. I was told that Officer Barley went over your options, and that's all the help we can give."

Again, we sit stunned. I thought with this last call our chances were better to force Mom into some type of help. I was wrong.

"Please, officer, there must be something you can do for us," my dad pleads. "I want my family back, and my kids need help more than ever now. Please, there HAS to be SOMETHING." His eyes well up with tears. If I didn't know it before, at that moment, my dad makes it abundantly clear there is nothing more important in the world than his family.

Again, I'm so sorry, sir. I really wish there was," Officer Cici responds. She is sincere, but it's not the answer we want.

Just as it seems that Diane's world has truly taken control, a glimmer of hope appears on the stairs as my mom sits at the top flipping my dad off. She is still drunk. Again, I quietly sneak upstairs and try to bait her into the living room. It works. Everyone, including the officers, looks stunned as my mom reappears.

"Diane, we had an agreement that you would go to bed. What are you doing down here?" Officer Cici asks.

"This is my house and I can do whatever the fuck I want," she barks back. To our luck, she had a little more liquid courage when she went upstairs.

"Don't get yourself arrested!" I tempt my mom. "You're getting close!"

"Fine, I'll just fucking kill myself then," Diane whispers under her breath so only I can hear.

"Why don't you say that a little louder for everyone to hear, Mom!" I demand, trying to get a rise out of her.

"Fine. I WANT TO KILL MYSELF! IS THAT WHAT EVERYONE WANTS TO HEAR!" Diane screams at the room. "I WANT TO KILL MYSELF!"

For the first time, the monster made a grave mistake, and I could not be happier. Tonight WILL be different.

"Diane, you have to come with me. I have no choice but to take you to the hospital to get you checked out by the doctors," Officer Cici commands.

"No, you can't take me anywhere. I REFUSE TO GO!" Diane answers.

"Once you're evaluated by the doctors, they will determine your next step, but it's out of our hands and yours," Officer Cici says as she grabs my mom's arm to direct her outside to the car. Diane squirms, so Officer Cici takes out a pair of handcuffs.

My dad intervenes. "Please don't use the handcuffs. She will go out to the car with you, but please don't use them."

At the same time, Diane lashes out in fear. She pushes the cop and swings her fist in her direction. Luckily, Officer Cici dodges, but now there is no debate. The handcuffs go on immediately.

With her hands behind her back, I grab my mom's arm to try and escort her to the car. As we walk towards the car, tears flow down her face. "Anthony, please save me. This is not how I want to do this. Please help me." It's my mom, not the monster.

Involuntarily, I start to tear up and respond, "I'm sorry, Mom. I'm here for you, I promise." I don't know what else to say, but I know the truth. I baited her into those handcuffs.

The walk down our driveway seems like an eternity as my mom cries and screams for me to help her. When the officer opens the back of the cop car, my mom squirms once again. Finally, she recognizes she has no choice and willingly sits in the seat.

The neighbors have come outside again and are watching from their front porches or windows like they are witnessing the final scene of a movie. I am so lost in my emotions that I don't notice them until my mom is in the car. I glance behind me and see my dad and sisters walking towards the car. Aubrey and Angie are crying too. My dad looks like he is having trouble keeping his emotions under control. My mom pleads for his help out of the open window.

"Elliot, I'm so sorry," she says softly as the cop car pulls away. "I love you! I love you, Elliot!"

And in an instant, she is gone.

Part III

Ascension

TEN

In My Life

My sisters, dad, and I are at a loss for words now that my mom has been taken away. We sit in silence as we all feel relieved for the first time in a long time. It is odd to not have our mom in the house. It is odd to sit in our living room without being stressed out. We each try to start a conversation but fall short, so we decide to process the situation, each in our own way. Concerned about what is happening with his wife, my dad leaves to meet with the doctors who will be evaluating my mom at the hospital. Aubrey and Angie turn on the TV and hang out with each other. I know they're going to talk about Mom and eventually call Grandma Palma to tell her everything. I decide to do what I do best: sit alone with my thoughts until I can make sense of how I feel.

I tell my sisters I'll be back and take the car. I drive along the Delaware River until I find a cutout in a road I've never noticed before. A big rock overlooks the dark abyss of the flowing water. I sit down and take a deep breath, and for the first time in a long time, I feel completely at ease. A cool breeze sweeps over the river and gently kisses my face. The night is truly beautiful. Living in a highly populated area, light pollution typically eats up most of our stars, but not tonight. This night, they all come out to brighten the gloomy day.

The mysterious tranquility of the water soothes me. The sounds of flowing water lapping at the bank ease me into quiet reflection. I cautiously enter my own head knowing it is both my best friend and my worst enemy.

"How am I supposed to understand all of this?" I whisper aloud. With that question, my mind takes me far away.

"Are you okay, honey?" my mom politely asked.

I nodded 'yes' but the tears running down my face screamed otherwise. We stood in the crowded parking between the six little league fields, my teammates walking by celebrating our victory with their parents smiling on. I pulled my hat down to try and hide my eyes, knowing they betrayed my feelings of worthlessness. "You know how your father gets when you play baseball. He wants you to be the best, but he tends to forget you're just a kid." Mom said, trying to comfort me.

"HE PULLED ME OUT OF THE ALL-STAR GAME AND SCREAMED AT ME SO EVERYONE COULD HEAR!" I yelled back through tears. I had held that anger in for the remainder of the game and through the 'talk' I had with my dad. Now I just had to let it out. "I NEVER WANT TO PLAY BASEBALL AGAIN!"

My mom walked up to me slowly and wrapped her arms around me. I was still shorter than her, but she knew it wouldn't be for much longer. She held onto me without any words until I settled down.

"I'm not trying to justify his actions," she said, "but your father acts like he does because he cares about you. A lot of people don't have someone like your dad that will be at every game, coach your team, and help you when you need it. He wants you to be a better baseball player than he was, but his passion gets the best of him at times. We all have our faults. Do you understand?"

I nodded my head yes, so she continued, "You are an excellent baseball player, and you're not going to quit. Instead, you will keep working with your dad and you will get better! Remember, can't is not in our vocabulary. And regardless of how you play, never forget that I am your number one fan."

Despite how bad I felt about the outcome of the game, I smiled. That bit of encouragement did not stop me from having bad games, nor did it stop my dad from letting his 'passion' get the best of him as he screamed at my smallest mistakes. But it did motivate me. No matter how tough the competition or practice became, I never considered quitting again.

When I reached my late teens and early twenties, my dad became my sage. His advice helped me immensely, and we developed a strong friendship on top of our typical father/son relationship. But growing up, I was a momma's boy, and the loving way in which my mom helped me through any situation was irreplaceable.

"Did you win?!" My dad asked with a hint of excitement.

I shrugged my shoulders, not sure how to answer. I was twelve years old and I had just had my first fist fight. The neighbors called my dad and he ran right over. A friend of mine had picked on me, so my temper took over and I punched him. I held my own, I think, but I felt wrong for fighting at all.

"Well, if somebody makes fun of you, you fight back. You have my full support!" my dad reassured me. I half-heartedly nodded. My dad glorified the fights he got into in his youth and his ability to use his fists to solve his issues when necessary. I thought I was like him in every aspect, but not this one.

When we walked in the door, my mom ran over to me like I had just survived a car crash. She checked every inch of me, paying close attention to the few bruises and red marks. She held me in a long embrace before my dad interrupted.

"Diane, he's a man. He's going to have fights. He has to defend himself one way or another," he said with a smile and a thumbs up.

My mom shook her head in disagreement. When my dad left the room, she took over.

"Are you really okay, honey?" she asked, concerned.

"Yeah… I'm okay…" I answered, looking at the ground.

"It didn't feel right, did it?" she asked as if she had read my mind. I shook my head 'no.'

She pulled me in for another long hug and started to give her famous advice: "Anthony, you're not a fighter. Your father may be, but you're not like him in this aspect. You're too sweet, whether you want to be or not. You're like your momma—a lover not a fighter. We are nice to everyone because we don't know what they may be going through. Just be yourself... My sweet boy doesn't need to get in any more fights."

Like usual, I smiled because she was right again.

That's the mother I will always remember—the woman who was there when we needed it most—the mother we loved and adored.

"Elliot! Elliot! Look on the news! It's the house we're staying in!" my Mom yelled.

It was seven in the morning, and my sisters, Taylor, and I were staying in a rental house in Ocean City, Maryland. But our relaxing summer trip went haywire when my mom called out to us that morning.

We all sleepily headed out of our separate bedrooms and into the living room to find out what all of the commotion was about. Just as we gathered around the TV, WHACK, the black boot of a large SWAT police officer connected with the wooden gate to the front yard busting it open, and two other officers hustled around the house and into the backyard.

We watched from the windows in shock as the first officer approached the front door in a bulletproof vest with a holstered pistol and an assault rifle at his side. Speechless, my dad opened the front door to meet the officer.

"Sir, do you own this house?" the officer asked, ignoring formalities.

"No, my family and I are renting it for the week. We just started our vacation," my dad answered.

The officer nodded and continued, "Have you seen any suspicious activity around the house?"

"No, not at all. We just woke—"

BANG! BANG! BANG! From the back of the house, a butt of a gun banged against wood loudly. The SWAT officer on the porch bolted in the direction of the noise. BANG! BANG! BANG! Panicked, my mom dove on the floor as if we were in the middle of a war. My sisters ran into their bedrooms, while Taylor and I froze because we didn't know how to react to the commotion.

Attempting to put on a brave face, my dad cautiously headed out the back door to figure out what had happened.

"Sir, why is this door locked?" another officer yelled to my dad while pointing the tip of his AR-15 at a storage shed in the backyard.

"I don't know. It was locked when we got here. The owner of this rental lives in the house next door if you need to get in," he responded.

The SWAT officer approached my dad again. "Listen, the bank at the corner of your street was robbed. We have reason to believe that the person who did it is hiding out around these houses. Lock your doors and stay away from the windows. The suspect is armed."

My dad nodded and headed back inside to tell the rest of us.

When he walked in, my mom was still laying on the floor. "Diane, what are you doing?" he asked with a smile.

"I don't know… Are we at war? Is there a terrorist?" she asked. Regardless of the situation, the questions Mom asked made us all laugh.

Then, my dad explained what the SWAT officer told him. "WHAT?! ELLIOT, WE HAVE TO GET OUT OF HERE!" Mom shockingly screamed.

In the front of the house, there were large windows exposing the entire living room. Without giving anyone else a chance to react, she jumped up and frantically began locking all of them. Then she ran to her bedroom.

"Mom, what are you doing?" I asked as she came out of the bedroom with her sheets.

"Help me out!" she yelled back.

Within minutes, the entire house was dark and fortified. The windows were completely covered by a combination of blankets, bedsheets, and tape. My mom even pushed the coffee table against the front door and stacked chairs on top of it, just in case the robber wanted to enter. Without many more materials for the back door, she 'stood guard.' "I'd rather him shoot me than get any of my children," she assured us. We laughed so hard at her antics we had tears in our eyes.

After fifteen minutes of sitting in the living room keeping one eye on the news and another on our mom, multiple SWAT officers knocked on the front door again. Not sure who it was, my mom dove on the floor again and low-crawled towards the door. Thank God the windows were blocked or we really would have looked suspicious. As we noticed other renters walking out to see what had happened, we all decided to walk out front to chat with the officers.

As it turned out, an armed man robbed the bank at the end of the street, but the teller gave him a wad of cash with a tracking device in it. As he saw cop cars approaching, he dropped the cash in the middle of the street by the house we were renting. The officers assured us they caught the only person responsible and that we were safe. The lead officer also apologized for the anonymous tip that had led them to check around our house.

As the officer was leaving, my mom's face was as white as a ghost.

"What's wrong, Mom?" Angie asked.

"I know why the officers checked our house…" she answered nervously.

"What? How do you know?" Dad asked.

"When I was walking the dog, I noticed the cash in the street. I picked it up and thought about bringing it home, but I ended up leaving it there. I guess somebody watched me and called the cops," she explained.

We all stared at her in disbelief, then laughed for a third time, harder than the others. Our mom's unintentional involvement in a bank heist was the highlight of that trip. Like my dad said, "It was a trip we'd remember for the rest of our lives."

"Oh, shit!" I yell out loud to no one in particular, snapping out of my thoughts as I remember my mom now won't be going with us on our first family trip to Disney World. Half of me wants to say 'she deserves it' and 'leave her, who cares?' The other half of me can't imagine the trip without her.

My mom lit up when I bought her a Disney shirt for the vacation, and after all the planning and excitement and buildup over the last year, our family would be incomplete without her there. A huge piece of us would be missing.

I leave the rock overlook, jump in my car and start the drive back home. I flip through the stations, and on the oldies station, I hear a familiar song.

"Na na na na, hey hey hey, boo bye!"

Growing up, my parents told me that was my favorite song. I couldn't say 'goodbye' so I replaced it with 'boo bye.' It was one of those silly things that children do that stick with parents years later. Recently, they said they'd put it on every once in a while because it reminded them of me.

I turn the song up and listen to it start to finish for the first time. What are the odds it would come on at the exact time I'm driving home after thinking about my mom? Everything happens for a reason. Mom's advice. For me, hearing that song on the way home is a sign.

I pull up to my house and notice all of the lights are still on even though it's after midnight. I walk inside to find my sisters sitting on the couch and my dad pacing around the living room. I sit down to join the conversation.

"I don't know if we should take her out of there, Dad," Aubrey says. "I don't want all of this to be for nothing."

I nod in agreement.

"I understand, but I feel horrible about what's happening to your mother," my dad says. "You guys didn't see the type of people in this place. She's being forced into a psychiatric hospital with the mentally insane. She's not nuts, she's an addict. The doctor I met with tonight plans on keeping her locked in her room like a prisoner, pumping medicine into her veins and having her go through a number of experimental therapies. Just based on my short experience there, I can only see it getting worse. We HAVE to get her out of there.

I nod at that, too.

"You're right," Aubrey says. "We can't leave her in a place that bad. Plus, she will miss our entire vacation."

"Yeah, but what if that's what she needs to get better and it makes her realize how bad her addiction is?" Angie counters. "It could end up being a good thing... I guess."

I nod again.

"Listen, guys. In the last thirty years, your mother and I have gone on every single vacation together. I love her and I can't leave your mom locked up being treated like a psychopath while we're having the trip of a lifetime without her. If she's not going, I'm not going." My dad drops this on us like a bomb. "I just can't do that to her. I can't!" He sits down not interested in explaining his position further.

Everyone turns their attention to me.

"I think we're damned if we do, damned if we don't," I say. "Mom has been wreaking havoc on us relentlessly lately and her addiction is to the point where it will kill her. Nevertheless, how beneficial will treatment at a facility like that be for Mom if her family is in Disney World having a great time without her? I don't know what the right move is. Only time will tell. All I know is that I love her and I can't imagine this vacation without her."

At that, we all sat in silence for a while until our dad spoke up.

"So here is the plan: we only have a few days before we are supposed to leave for vacation. We'll visit her the next couple of days and talk to the doctors about treatment. Then, if we can, we'll set up an outpatient program for your mother that starts THE DAY we get home from Disney World—something in a legitimate rehabilitation center. That way she goes willingly, under the right conditions, and she won't be missing a big event that would make her want to leave. As for her addiction, we'll watch her the whole trip to make sure she can't slip up. Does everyone agree?"

Aubrey and I nod in agreement.

"Let's save mom," Angie concurs.

"Let's save mom!" my dad repeats with a smile.

I walk upstairs; the same stairs I'd run up and down relentlessly as a kid. Somehow I feel drawn to my parents' bedroom. After the day we just had, I know it will look like a crime scene, but at the moment, I'm pulled into that room for a different reason: nostalgia. As a kid, I often jumped into my parent's bed. There was a certain level of comfort with them that always pulled me in. I felt warm and safe. Now, cigarette ashes stain the floor leaving a strong odor, and the sheets on the bed haven't been cleaned in weeks. Since my dad moved out of the room, it hasn't been taken care of.

Regardless of the mess, the mirrors over the headrest still act as a mantle for numerous childhood pictures and family mementos. Taped to the corner is a poem I wrote at my senior year high school graduation. As a number of students read speeches about their years in school and performed their many talents one last time before we entered the 'real world,' I sat in my chair in thought. I laughed and cried with everyone the whole night. When I rose to walk by my mom in my cap and gown to receive my diploma, I saw her cry. When I returned to my seat, I took out my phone and wrote the following poem:

It's the first day of school and the sun is shining high
Moms holding tight, she doesn't want to say bye
She kneels down to her son's height and starts to cry
Why mommy why? Why must you cry?
My baby's leaving the nest, he's starting to fly
A stern voice interrupts and says, "He's in good hands"
I know. Don't grow up too fast on me until I'm picking up a man!
Mommy loves you and will be counting down the minutes until she sees you again.

Nine years go by like the blink of an eye
The baby is now a boy
Trading in his toys for a football and a deeper voice
Braces on his teeth, acne on his face
High school knocking at the gate
Mommy turns into 'mom' who only gets calls for rides
His curfew's at 10, but he never arrives on time
He only comes home to eat and sleep
On the last day of school, his mom weeps
Why mom why? Why must you cry?
My baby's leaving the nest, he's flying high
Don't grow up too fast so I come home to a man!
Mommy loves you and will be counting down the minutes until
she sees you again.

Four years pass like the blink of an eye
High school is ending, it's time to say goodbye
The baby is now a young man
With a plan in his hands
Top of his class, moving on to dreams
A world unknown not as easy as it seems
After the diploma comes jobs and bills
Filled with responsibilities and hardships, not as many thrills
Mom becomes 'Ma,' who only gets calls for meals
Son now has a job, a girlfriend, and a license to get behind the
wheel.

Graduation passes by like the blink of an eye
Son sees his mom crying and asks, Why ma why? Why must
you cry?
My baby's leaving the nest, he's soaring so high
I can't stay strong any longer
I want my baby back, back to being a boy

Back to crying loud, which I could cure with tickles of joy
Back to needing me all hours of the day
Back to listening to every word I say.

The son answers promptly, tears in his eyes
Mom no matter what, we will always be by each other's sides
It's hard to grow up, hard leaving the nest
But with your love, I learned how to be the best
Every time you can't see me
Look into your heart and you will find
All of our great memories and the ties that bind.
She wipes away her tears and looks into his eyes
She says, Mommy loves you and will be counting down the
minutes until she sees you again.
And in the blink of an eye, life passed by.

As I read the last line, I whisper aloud, "Let's save mom."

ELEVEN

Broken Halos

"Diane? Diane, are you okay?"

She looks at him with empty eyes and doesn't answer.

"Diane, can you answer me so I know you're alright?" my dad tries again.

"Hi… Elliot…" she finally responds. The words tumble out of her mouth as if she isn't the one who said them. Her eyes remain staring off in the distance.

They are in the visitors' area of Bronze Oaks Mental Health Center surrounded by other patients catching up with loved ones—some young, some old, all lost. My dad and Aubrey find a secluded place in the corner to talk to Mom. The visitation room is small with blocks and other children's games; it resembles a waiting room at a pediatrician's office, but there are no children to be found.

"We only have fifteen minutes to talk today, so we want to see how everything is going here. How are you feeling?" my dad asks.

My mom stares at the wall and draws her answer out long and slow, "Hi... Angie... I... didn't... see... you... there."

Aubrey and my dad look at each other baffled. "Um, mom, Angie isn't here," Aubrey tells her.

My mom's eyebrows scrunch up as she looks past them at no one. "Yes... she is. She's... right there," my mom states with more confidence, but she is pointing at a white wall. "Come here... Angie. Sit... with... me."

More confused than before, my dad attempts to break my mom out of whatever trance she is in. "Diane, look at me. Angie's not here, it's just Aubrey and I. Focus.".

Still dazed, my mom looks in their direction. "Whatever... you... say...Elliot. I'm... not... blind," she says.

Ignoring the jab, my dad begins questioning her to understand the situation better, "Do you know what kind of medicine they gave you?" he asks.

My mom stares at them for what seems like a full minute before she answers, "Um... I know... something... for... depression. The doctor... had... me... drink... alcohol... and gave... me... medicine for.... my drinking."

"WHAT?!" my dad yells at her loud enough for everyone to turn their attention their way. "Alcohol?! What for?"

Before he can get an answer, a nurse steps in and announces the visitation period is over. Without saying anything, my mom stands up and starts to walk towards her room.

"Diane, wait!" my dad calls out to her. She turns slowly and stares at him. He walks over to her and brings her in for a long embrace. "Hang in there, cookie. We're here for you and we're going to do right by you. You can get through this," he whispers in her ear before he gives her a kiss.

Tears in her eyes, Diane turns and heads out of sight down a bright corridor. My dad wipes his own eyes and turns around just in time to see a small older doctor heading out of his office—a different doctor from the one he spoke with the night before.

Excuse me, doctor, my wife was just admitted here, and I had a couple of quick questions for you," he says.

The man turns but looks as if he doesn't want to be bothered. Still looking down at his paperwork, he asks, "Who is your wife?"

Diane Mazzani She was just admitted yesterday," my dad replies.

"Ah, yes. What do you want to know?" the doctor asks, still looking down.

Noticing the man doesn't want to be bothered, my dad jumps to the most important question, "What medicine is my wife on? She seemed completely out of it and was hallucinating."

"Can't tell you," the doctor answers without looking up. "I'm assuming you spoke with another doctor last night. He told you all you need to know."

"Listen, I'm her husband and I'd like to know why my wife is hallucinating and can barely speak after one day of being in this place. Tell me what you are giving her!" my dad demands.

Finally, the doctor looks up at my dad. He is at least a head shorter and much plumper. "Sir, I can't tell you what we're giving your wife. That is between her and her doctors. Are you done?"

"No, I'm not done!" my dad yells, his face turning red with anger as he takes a step closer. "When my wife seems brain dead and tells me her doctor is forcing her to drink alcohol, it's my business too. Why the fuck are you having an alcoholic drink more alcohol a day after being forced in here?!"

The confrontation catches the attention of some of the nurses and other assistants.

Startled, the doctor takes a few steps back. "We wean addicts off of their drug here," he responds. "That's all I will tell you. Your wife doesn't have a choice."

My dad looks ready to explode. His fists are clenched and his eyes pierce the small doctor's skull. My dad takes a breath to calm down. He has the doctor's attention, so he might as well make the best of it rather than causing a scene. "I'll be honest with you, my wife does not deserve to be here," my dad starts. The doctor rolls his eyes as if he hears it every day, but my dad ignores him and continues. "She has a problem, but it is with addiction, not a mental issue. We forced her in here and, because of that, she is going to miss something really important to all of us. Are there any other options we can discuss?"

The doctor looks back down, this time more nervously. "No, your wife needs to stay in here. Our methods work. There's nothing to discuss."

All my dad's anger floods back into him. "What the fuck do you mean there's nothing to discuss? I'm asking to sit down and talk about options and you won't even grant me that? Who the fuck do you think you are?!" he yells losing his cool again.

"No, no options. This is the only option," the doctor answers, slowly backing away.

"What the fuc—" my dad starts again but stops as the doctor runs away scattering papers behind him. He slams his office door, and soon after, two security guards run up to my dad as Aubrey looks on.

"Sir, we received a distress call about you. Visiting hours are over and you made your point. It's time to leave," the large security guard demands.

Aubrey and Dad leave the building feeling angry and confused. "We need to save mom," Aubrey says.

While they're away, Ang and I run some errands to get ready for our vacation. When Aubrey and Dad return, we intently listen to every word of their experience at the mental hospital. It's unbelievable, and Ang and I both agree we need to get Mom out of there.

The next day, Angie, my dad, and I wake up at seven in the morning and drive 45 minutes to an area we've never been. We pull up to a large old brick building with no signs. Without a GPS, it would be nearly impossible to find. Tucked away amongst a number of office buildings, the mental facility blends in with its surroundings as if to look as inconspicuous as possible.

"Leave your cell phones in the car," my dad directs. "They'll confiscate them at the door if you don't. You're not going to believe this place when you experience it; it's like One Flew Over the Cuckoo's Nest in there!"

We take the reference to heart and stick our phones in the glove compartment, but I put a small journal and pen in my pocket. I want to jot down exactly what I observe.

We approach the front door to the obscure building where a line has formed. We stand in the back and wait. Through an outside speaker, a lady announces the beginning of family visitation, and a loud buzz plays through the speaker as the door mechanically unlocks. The family in front of the line follows the directions as though they've done it a hundred times.

We walk through two sets of locked, thick, bulletproof-glass doors before approaching a long desk crowded with hospital staff. With roughly forty people coming to see their loved ones, we wait in line for about ten minutes before we reach the assembly line of secretaries and nurses all tasked with visitor entry. The first person is a security guard. He pats us down and has us explain anything in our pockets.

"Sir, what is in your left pocket?" he asks me in a deep voice.

"It's just a notebook and a pen," I answer tentatively.

"Remove the items," he commands.

I do as he says and hold them in front of me for him to see. Behind me, people are making remarks about us holding up the line.

"This item is not allowed," he says placing a finger on the notebook. "Please dispose of the item before continuing into the building." I nod my head and remove myself from the line. My dad hands me the keys to our car, and I head towards the exit baffled by the strict policy.

Before I leave, I notice a large decorated sign behind the front desk staff. It reads: "Those who wander are lost; our hands put them back on the path of righteousness." I quickly jot the words of the sign down and head back to the car.

I drop off my notebook and head back inside for more of the dog-and-pony show. The security guard checks me again, then signals me to the next employee. I sign a waiver agreeing not to document or post online anything about the facility or what I observe. The next employee scans my ID, then prints out a visitor's pass. I reach the end of the table and sign my name next to my mom's to affirm why I'm there. A weird sensation pours over me. Almost every day for the last few years I hoped we'd be in this position. Now, I hope to get her name off of this clipboard as soon as possible. I forced her into a psych ward against her will and feel nothing but remorse.

The facility is like something out of The Giver. Every sign, every employee, and every action is done methodically and under control. Without cell phones, cameras, or even notebooks, the inner workings remain a secret between the employees and the people in charge. The patients can't use phones, so any outside communication other than the fifteen minutes during visitation is prohibited. I have an odd feeling that family members of the patients have accepted their fate because they were forced into the facility out of desperation. Maybe it's a last resort for them, but not for us.

Finally, a few nurses herd me into a waiting room with all of the other families. Like a tour group at a museum, we're whisked up a flight of stairs and down a corridor in complete silence.

We reach a small room to our right and our 'guides' direct us to all file in and find seats. I did not believe my dad when he first described the room, but it is completely unfitting for the situation. Bean bags, small chairs, bead-tables, and a chalk wall. Why is a visitation center of an adult mental facility set up like a daycare? I wonder.

The patients file into the room one after another, and family members stand and embrace their loved ones. Out of the corner of my eye, one patient stands out from the rest—a fifteen-year-old boy I recognize. I stare at him until it dawns on me I had a Science class with him in high school. He was a few years younger than me but was well known and talkative. Now, his eyes are sunken in, he's extremely thin, and he has a blank expression on his face. He stares off in the distance, a single tear rolling down his face as his mom holds him.

Out of curiosity, I try to listen in but only catch bits and pieces of what his mom says: "Your dad couldn't make it. You know he wanted... only twenty-seven more days... You look better... brought your favorite hoodie... you'll be healthier when you get out... I love you so much..."

Eventually, they move to the other side of the room, and I can't hear them anymore. Still, I look on, stunned. The whole time the boy was in his mom's arms, he did not say a word. He simply remained motionless as she took the lead in the conversation. I hope he can find his way out of this shit. I hope we can find a way out.

Before I can observe too many of the other patients, my dad nudges Angie and I. "Let's get out of this room. It's too stuffy and your mom isn't even here yet."

It doesn't seem like she is coming.

My dad isn't fazed when a nurse tries to stop him from leaving the room. Instead, he pulls us into the hall and demands that his wife is brought to visitation. He argues with a few nurses and persists until my mom turns a corner and walks slowly down the bright corridor.

Her eyes are wide open as she approaches us like a zombie. Upon reaching us, she starts to cry. "The doctor... told me... you guys... weren't coming... to... see me." She drags out her words, but it seems better than my dad described the day before.

My dad grinds his teeth, "When did they tell you that?!"

Ignoring the question, my mom walks in my direction with tears streaming down her face. "Anthony... I thought... you hated me...," she cries.

Swelling with the emotional memories of my youth, I start to tear up as I hug my mom. "I told you I was going to save you," I say with a small smile. We're doing the right thing trying to take her out.

"Diane, are you sure the doctor said that?" my dad pushes for an answer.

"Ye-yes... he told me... that my family... was not coming," she replies confidently.

My dad leaves us to speak to a group of nurses at a desk a few feet away. My mom makes her way to Angie to hug her. Angie asks about the hallucinations from the day before, but our mom has no recollection. After short pleasantries and reassuring promises we can't guarantee, we all stand in the hallway in awkward silence. As much as we love our mom, we can't come up with the right words at the moment. Looking for a distraction, I hear screaming coming from a hallway to my right.

"HELP ME! GET ME OUT OF THIS GODFORSAKEN PLACE! HELP ME!" a man yells while walking towards me. He is middle-aged with shaggy, brown hair, a long beard, and every part of his body trembles at different times. In another setting, I would assume he was homeless. Here, he is just another 'lost soul.'

Out of complete awkwardness, I feel obligated to respond. "What's wrong?" I ask with as much sincerity as I can muster.

"This place... THIS PLACE... I can't take it anymore... THIS PLACE IS DRIVING ME INSANE!" he wails.

I am too taken aback to answer. Fortunately, two large male nurses rush over and grab the disheveled man by his arms. "Are you going to settle down?" one nurse asks.

"AAAAAAAAHHHHHHHH! LET ME OUT OF HERE! THEY WON'T LET ME OUT! LET ME OUT

OF HERE!" the man screeches while kicking at his captors. Another male nurse walks over calmly and administers a needle. Instantly, the yelling and kicking stop. The fight drains out of the man, and he is dragged back down another bright corridor.

The scene has everyone's attention, but after a few minutes, everything settles back down.

"That's... Gene. He's really...scary," my mom says. "He doesn't seem... all there... if you know what... I mean. I don't know why... but he comes in... my room asking... if I'm married... I really don't like it," she adds quietly.

"And he's allowed to?" Ang is astonished.

"The nurses... they shrug it off..." she responds hesitantly.

Trying to get as much information as I can, I push my mom to delve deeper into what else happens in the facility.

"They have you do... weird exercises... I can't call you... no matter how much I ask... Sometimes I can't... leave my room... sometimes I ask for... people to leave... but they don't have to. The nurses... they're mean... but the doctor... he's worse. He said he's keeping me... until he says I'm ready..." She pauses as tears run down her face. "Anthony, I don't want to... talk about it anymore."

Something must have happened to cause her to break down like this. I want to know more, but deciding to respect my mom's wishes, I nod and give her another hug.

Throughout all of the commotion, my dad argues with the nurses just out of earshot. We know he is demanding to see the doctor, and when he returns to us, we can tell they've refused. Before we know it, the time is up.

"The visitation period is over. Families, please line up at the door as we will be leaving promptly," a nurse commands.

Without any further argument, my dad brings my mom in for another long embrace. "Listen, cookie, you will be out of here no matter what. I absolutely promise you that."

"Are you serious?" My mom asks in disbelief while crying hysterically.

"I promise… I love you, Diane," he responds with a reassuring smile.

We give our mom a hug as she turns and walks down the long, bright hallway. Tears roll down my face as we walk away. I can't hold my emotions in any longer. No matter the insults, despite the breakdowns, headaches, and heartaches she's caused in the past, I just long for my mom back to be back with us. We are so close, and yet I feel helpless and totally out of control. I know we have to fight to bring her home.

We are definitely doing the right thing. We have to get her out.

My dad, Ang, and I follow the 'tour group' out of the building until we can break off and head to our car. Once inside, my dad finally outlines the severity of the case.

"That fucking doctor locked himself in his room and claimed he was with a patient the entire time. I'm not stupid, I know what he's doing!" my dad complains loudly. He takes a breath and calms down. "I have a plan. I'm going to get in touch with my cousin who is a lawyer. She doesn't work on these cases, but maybe she knows a few people that can help us out. I'll see if there is a legal way to pull Mom out of there. Just threatening to use a lawyer could push the doctor to let her out; it's obvious they don't want people knowing everything that goes on in there. And if that doesn't work, we're breaking her out!"

We all laugh at the image of the four of us trying to break Mom out of the facility. It feels nice to be acting as a family again… It feels nice to truly love our mom again.

Once we return home, my dad spends the next six hours on the phone with a notebook and pen in his hand. My sisters and I spend the time packing our mom's clothes and necessities for the trip. We go to a few stores to buy her new hats, t-shirts, and shoes—all the while singing along to Disney songs. It is the first time in a while we've prepared to do something as a family without worrying how disastrous it could be.

After a long day, we all close our eyes for the night, eagerly anticipating our mother's triumphant return.

"ANTHONY! ANTHONY, WHERE ARE YOU?!" I wake up to my mom wailing. I jump out of bed shocked to hear her voice. I push my sisters' bedroom door open, but neither of them are in their room. Nobody is making noise from downstairs, so I burst through my parent's bedroom door.

In the middle of the room stands my mom with blood soaking her white shirt. She has a large slash across her chest and her face is as pale as a ghost. A large kitchen knife drops to the floor as her body goes limp. I run over to catch her before she collapses.

"Mom, what happened? How did you get home?" I ask, trying to understand how this could have happened.

"Dad p-picked me up this mor-morning from that place. Your s-s-sisters and he went out to get the re-rental car," she answers through sobs.

"None of that matters right now. You need help! What did you do?!" I panic.

My mom's hysterical crying somehow materializes into an answer, "I d-d-drank w-when they le-left. I c-c-can't do it an-anymore."

She falls faint in my arms and her eyes close. I bring us both down to our knees to rest her head against my chest. I HAVE to call an ambulance immediately. Before I can move, the entire room turns black, and a deep dark voice snickers in my ear. "I will always win. She will never be able to escape my grasp." The voice stops, and my vision comes back, but my mom is gone. I'm left kneeling in a pool of blood. "MMOOOOMM HHEEELLLPPP UUUUUSSSS! MMOOOOMM!" I scream at the top of my lungs, but no one answers.

"Ant! Ant!" Angie yells. "Wake up!"

I roll over in my bed to see my sister standing over me. "Dad just called. He'll be home in a few minutes."

I sit up sweating and confused. Another bad dream… Thank god.

"Guys, come downstairs!" my dad calls up to us. We run down like it's Christmas morning. "We saved Mom," he says with a huge smile. Next to him stands my mom with joyful tears pouring out of her eyes and a smile bigger than her face.

I know how she feels. After that nightmare, I can't be happier to see her walk through the front door. I grab her and hold her in a long embrace.

"I love you so much, Anthony," my mom whispers. "I'm so sorry. This will NEVER happen again. I swear to god this will never happen again."

I grin from ear to ear. "I know it won't, Mom. I love you so much."

TWELVE

Too Good to be True

"You're just too good to be true
Can't take my eyes off of you
You'd be like heaven to touch
I wanna hold you so much
At long last love has arrived
And I thank God I'm alive
You're just too good to be true
Can't take my eyes off of you."

My parents sing in unison to an embarrassed Angie.
And when the song hits the chorus, they both start to do
their best Frankie Valli impression at the top of their
lungs:

"I love you, baby!
And if it's quite alright, I need you baby
To warm the lonely nights, I love you baby
Trust in me when I say
Oh pretty baby

Don't bring me down I pray
Oh pretty baby, now that I've found you stay
And let me love you, baby
Let me love you!"

Pointing and dancing around her the whole time, they finish their driveway performance by each landing a big kiss on Angie's red cheeks. Aubrey and I feel awkward too, but we can't help but laugh. When the chorus hits again, we all sing along—even Angie.

The van is packed, and we can't wait to begin our journey to Disney World. My dad calls it, "The family trip we'll remember for the rest of our lives."

Taylor and I sit on the first bench seat of the van. With Aubrey's selfie stick, Taylor takes a picture to commemorate the beginning of our journey. Behind us in the middle row sits Angie and her boyfriend; they couldn't look more eager as it's both of their first times going to Disney World. In the last row of the van sits Aubrey, her boyfriend, and our dog, Bella. They look tired, but happy. In the front seats are my parents. My dad is glowing and next to him, shining the brightest is our mom. She's with her family, she's sober, and the problems of the days leading up to our trip are now in the past. We all smile from ear to ear. We're headed to our favorite place in the world and our family is all here.

Even though we're in the car for twenty hours, the ride to Florida never feels shorter.

Neither the traffic nor the thunderstorms ruin our happiness. The house we rented has four large bedrooms, a jacuzzi tub, and a personal pool. We're going to paradise.

For the first three days of our vacation, it pours, but we don't let the rain bother us. Instead, we drive out to different beaches until, as my dad puts it, we "find the sun." As if rewarded for our diligence, we have perfect weather the rest of the week.

The magic of Disney World touches each of us as we walk down Main Street towards Cinderella's castle in the Magic Kingdom. We stop in front of Mickey and Walt for a picture—the 'Fantastic Five' together again. The euphoria our family feels is almost indescribable. It's like for a long time we had lost our mom and there was a big hole in our hearts, and now magically she has reappeared as the beautiful, loving, funny, and caring person she always was.

Whether it is walking around the parks, riding the roller coasters, or watching the fireworks, every little part of the trip is fantastic. We joke, laugh, and love without a care in the world.

Later in the week, we jump back in the van to drive to St. Pete's for a day in the sun. My dad shows us his old college campus and takes us to a spot on the beach he remembers frequenting in his youth. It's the first time we've been to the west side of Florida and had a chance to swim in the Gulf of Mexico, so we all look forward to seeing the crystal-clear water.

"Ew, this water is green just like the Jersey Shore," Ang says disappointed once we arrive.

To our surprise, the storms earlier in the week brought debris and bacteria to the shore. The sand and water are both covered in it.

"Oh well, at least we're here!" I respond with optimism.

We set up camp on the crowded beach and relax the day away. After some time, Aubrey and her boyfriend go on a walk to find seashells while Angie and her boyfriend look for a bathroom to deal with the stomach bug he caught the day before. Taylor and I leave the beach to find a cool place to eat. We walk around for about twenty minutes and find a perfect restaurant advertising the best burgers in town. When we walk back to our spot, I notice my dad sitting alone.

"Where's Mom?" I ask calmly.

"She just left to go to the bathroom," he answers with his eyes shut and head tilted towards the sun.

I sit for a second, but I'm suddenly restless. Angie and her boyfriend return, but without Mom.

"Ang, did you see Mom?" I ask with a growing apprehension.

"No, why?" she responds.

Not trying to make anyone anxious, I make up an excuse, "I was just wondering. Dad said she went to the bathroom. But maybe she went to find a new beach towel. Hers is really old."

A sense of dread pours over me. I whisper to Taylor that I'm going to find Mom, and not to tell anybody else.

I head to the bathroom and stand outside for a few minutes, but Mom never comes out. I walk around the beach shop, but I don't have any luck there either. Like a magnet, my eyes move to the giant sign that reads, "Larry's Beach Bar and Grill."

As I look across the street, I see a large, round bar with a few patrons and one bartender. A lady attempting to be as inconspicuous as possible signals him over.

"Please, it can't be her. Please, God, don't let it be her," I say aloud.

I venture closer to the bar, shaking with panic just in time to see my mom gulp down a glass of straight vodka.

A familiar dark voice whispers in my ear, "She'll always be mine…"

Thank you for purchasing this book. A portion of the book's proceeds will be donated to the national addiction and mental health foundation, "To Write Love on Her Arms." Their mission statement is as follows: "To Write Love on Her Arms is a non-profit movement dedicated to presenting hope and finding help for those who are struggling with depression, addiction, self-injury, and suicide. TWLOHA exists to encourage, inform, inspire, and invest directly into treatment and recovery."

For more information, please visit twloha.com

EPILOGUE (SAVE MYSELF)

Angie's high-pitched screams echoed through the halls many more times as my mom's alcoholism brought about more surprises. She nearly bled out in her bed from a head injury she sustained in a drunken fall, was sent to the hospital four times for unrelated accidents, and had another forced stint in a rehabilitation facility. Nevertheless, my family and I still find ourselves at a loss as to how to deal with her addiction.

A year after our trip to Florida, we decided to break our old routine. I graduated college and moved back home until I could afford to live on my own. I started a job teaching Social Studies at my old high school. Unfortunately, some of my students lived in my neighborhood and experienced my mom's drunken antics. But it was worse than that. During those six months in the house, I felt helpless as I was again barraged with insults and forced to watch my mom slowly killing herself. As much as I loved her and my family, I needed to do something for me before the stresses of a new job and student loan debt and worry over my mom's endless problems drove me insane. So, after a fifth visit from the cops in one month and a screaming match outside of our house, I decided to move in with Taylor. Doing so helped me distance myself from my mom's addiction, vastly improving my mental health.

My decision must have resonated with my family because they soon followed my lead. Shortly after I left, Aubrey started a new relationship and moved in with her boyfriend. My dad and Angie stuck around the house for a few months longer before finding their own small apartment.

Despite moving out, my dad remains my mom's caretaker. Almost every day, he checks up on her. He also provides her with food and money regardless of how much she wastes both of them. Angie is still hurt and bitter. As long as my mom continues to drink, she will not speak to her. Aubrey takes a different approach: she spends a small amount of time each day visiting and talking with my mom. I think it brings both her and my mom a little bit of solace.

I find myself in between my sisters' approaches. Some days I want to see my mom and spend time with her. Other days, I avoid the situation altogether—not even bothering to call. But I still worry about her every day.

Recently, a family friend died from alcoholism. The despair in their loved ones' eyes broke my heart. Now, on my way home from work each day, I pass the house I grew up in and cry, wondering if today will be my mom's last.

Sober, my mom is distraught but aware that her alcoholism led to her living alone in our house. She spends most of her time attempting to make a few dollars at a local warehouse doing odd jobs and talking to our family about her intentions of staying sober. When she is drunk, she is still bitter and nasty, blaming anyone else for her predicament. When she is like that, we no longer have to run away; we simply avoid the house. Both sober and drunk, my mom holds steady to the belief that she can overcome her addiction on her own and that she doesn't need professional help. I hope she proves us all wrong… But after all the calls to crisis centers, hotlines, and psychiatrists, I feel we are running out of time.

Death comes like a thief in the night, stealing what we all cherish most. For some, he moves swiftly, snatching life all at once. With others, he takes them piece by piece under the false pretenses that finality isn't approaching. Though suicide seems like the former, it is really the latter. With suicide, death gives no guarantees. On the contrary, he leaves those with depression the slim chance to rewrite their ending. And if one escaped death's clutches, it may only be temporary. Still, it is worth trying.

ACKNOWLEDGMENTS

To my amazing family who has stuck by me no matter what. To my grandma, for her never-ending support, my dad for being my best friend, my sisters for making me a better man, my friends for always having my back, my fiancé for loving me unconditionally, and finally my mom for instilling in me values I'll never lose and for proving that "can't is not in our vocabulary." A special thank you to my editor, Dustin Schwindt, for making this book possible, Andrew Arcangeli for creating a beautiful logo, SpettaDesigns (Ron Clarkson) for the fantastic cover, and Mark Lefebvre for all of his help after the completion of the book.

Made in the USA
Columbia, SC
22 December 2018